# The
# School Governor's
# Legal Guide

## Chris Lowe

**Croner Publications Ltd**
Croner House
173 Kingston Road
New Malden
Surrey KT3 3SS
Tel: 01 942 8966

Published by
Croner Publications Ltd.,
Croner House,
173 Kingston Road,
New Malden,
Surrey KT3 3SS
Telephone 01-942 8966

While every care has been taken
in the writing and editing of this book,
readers should be aware that only Acts of Parliament
and Statutory Instruments have the force of Law,
and that only the courts can authoritatively
interpret the law.

British Library Cataloguing in Publication Data
A CIP Catalogue Record for this book
is available from the British Library


ISBN 0 900319 59 3


Set in Linotype Plantin
and printed by
Adlard & Son Ltd.,
Dorking,
Surrey.

SB 39916(2)/6 . 11·88

# Contents

# Foreword

Governors could hardly be blamed for feeling confused and uncertain about their legal duties and obligations. They are constantly being told that they must undertake new responsibilities, and yet in their own schools they may well find considerable resistance to the new style of governing, both from the Head and from their fellow governors. Although the changes introduced by the 1986 Act will not be fully implemented until September 1988 for county schools or September 1989 for voluntary schools, the extensive media coverage of Kenneth Baker's Education Reform Bill gives rise to more confusion. Many of its provisions will, if they become law, supersede the 1986 Act. They are not planned, however, to come into force before the 1990s.

So it will be a great advantage for governors to be able to refer to this succinct, straightforward, easily accessible guide to current education law. No more arguments about legal liability, health and safety, control of admissions, and the finer points of the composition of governing bodies, or the differences between county and voluntary schools. A quick reference to the *Legal Guide* will settle them all — insofar as they can be settled, because of course the letter of the law is not always a help when it comes to defining the relationships on which successful school governing depends.

Mr Lowe has rightly avoided any attempt to produce a guide to being a good governor — plenty of those are already on the market. However, governors will be more effective for being able to rely on an authoritative guide to the law. Governor trainers too, often expected to be experts on a wide range of legal topics, will find it a valuable resource, not to speak of the professionals themselves, who often have a very hazy idea of what the law says.

There is an unfortunate trend at present towards investing the governor's job with great mystique. To listen to some of the pundits, you would think that every governor has to be an accountant, an architect and a fully paid up member of the Institute of Personnel Management. This is to misunderstand the whole purpose of having lay governors, whose value lies precisely in their non-professional status. We pay the professionals to do a professional job, but schools must be accountable to the community they serve, and the vehicle for this accountability is the lay governing body.

To do their job well, governors must have an interest in the school, commonsense and confidence in the value of their contribution. They don't need to know everything about the law, or the curriculum, or finance or anything else, but they do need to know where to find independent, usable information on these topics, when they want it. With the right kind of help, we can look forward to a genuine partnership of school, staff, parents, pupils and governors, that can only benefit our education system.

Felicity Taylor
April 1988

# Introduction

This book does not set out to teach governors, or those intending to be governors, how to do the job. There are other books and resources that should be consulted for that purpose.

The aim of this book is to inform the reader, in an easy-to-read and succinct form, of the legal background of school government. It does not, therefore, offer opinion or personal comment, although the reader's attention is often drawn to the implications of the law, and to the complications involved, when so many different parties — Central Government, Department of Education and Science officials, Her Majesty's Inspectors, Local Education Authorities, local community, governors, parents, Heads and teachers — have rights, powers and duties in the course of educating the nation's youth.

The law of education is contained in many Acts of Parliament from which flow Statutory Instruments (ie regulations made by the Secretary of State by virtue of powers given to him in an Act), Circulars and Administrative Memoranda (which are explanations of, or guidance to, the law and regulations) and cases decided in the Courts. It is continually evolving, both through statutes and case law.

The Education (No.2) Act 1986 has established a new partnership between parents, local authorities, the community and staff through new governing bodies, and in addition has spelt out the considerable commitments and accountabilities placed on governors. These will be further increased when the Education Reform Bill 1987 becomes law. The provisions of the Bill are known and are taken into account in this book. But clearly all law books can only capture the law as it stands at one moment in time. The law expounded here refers mainly to schools in England and Wales, and wherever possible, Northern Ireland, as known at the time of writing.

I will permit myself one personal observation which I hold to with some passion. It is this — schools at the end of the day are not about governors' legal duties nor Heads' responsibilities, nor about teachers' rights or parents' rights, nor about the Secretary of State's or LEAs' powers; they are about children's learning, learning both for the here and now, as growing children and then as young people, and also as preparation for life after school. The legal requirements for governorship should always, it seems to me, be subservient to the ultimate ends of school education.

This is why much of education law is couched in what appears to be unhelpfully vague generalities — "governors should have regard to . . .", "having consulted . . .", "governors should take reasonably practicable steps to . . .", "governors must take steps to ensure that . . ." We should in fact be grateful that this flexibility allows LEAs, governors, Heads and teachers the liberty to look to the particular needs of particular schools.

Governors in discharging their duties will need to know their schools as well as possible and to seek to guide the Head and staff, while not interfering with their professional responsibilities. A knowledge of the legal framework, what is and what is not permissible, will add an essential dimension to the governor's expertise. It is no substitute, however, for the application of commonsense and experience that the new governing bodies should have at their disposal.

# Acknowledgements

I should like to thank all those colleagues and governors who have helped to shape the format of this book and Daphne Willis, my secretary, for deciphering my handwriting and typing the manuscript.

I am grateful also for the helpful comments of those who critically reviewed the draft copy, namely, Richard Cunningham, Secretary of the Catholic Education Council; Dora Loftus, Chairman of Governors, Burntwood School, ILEA and Felicity Taylor, Editor of "School Governor" the journal of the National Association of Governors and Managers. The advice and assistance of Anthony Woodard, editor of Croner's Head's Legal Guide was also greatly appreciated.

# Background to School Government

**1**

## A HISTORY

School governors as we have come to know them were first introduced in the early part of the nineteenth century to inspect the schools set up by the National Society and the British and Foreign Schools Society with government grants. ˙

Late in the century the Public Schools Act and Endowed Schools Act enhanced the role of these boards of managers and, following the Education Act 1870 (the Forster Act), school boards could be elected in districts which were considered to be deficient in elementary schools. These boards had powers to delegate some of their responsibilities to boards of managers of individual schools. Through the 1880s and 1890s the school boards' responsibilities were enhanced as public elementary education grew.

### THE 1902 ACT

The Education Act 1902 marked the next major step. It set up the system of local education authorities which in the main still exists and made provision for secondary schools as well as elementary schools. All elementary schools had to have "school managers", and secondary schools could have "governors" although these were resisted by many local authorities who saw no reason for delegating their responsibilities. This attitude actually persisted until the 1980 Act in some areas where large numbers of schools were grouped under one Governing Body dominated by local authority representatives.

### THE 1944 ACT

From the 1902 Act onwards, school governors (the term "manager" was abolished by the 1980 Act) have had local responsibility for the welfare and progress of individual schools and their powers and duties were further increased by the Education Act 1944. Sections 17 and 19 of this Act required each school to have a governing body, the constitution of which could be set out in an Instrument of Government and its duties and responsibilities in Articles of Government. However, for many reasons governors' interest and involvement became on the whole superficial and tended more to ceremonial than educational matters. Heads became very powerful because few of the checks set out in the Model Articles of Government, following the 1944 Act, were ever invoked even if governors actually knew about them.

The advent of comprehensive schools and growing parental interest in schools led to further changes being advocated by the Taylor Committee in the mid 1970s. The Committee report *A New Partnership for our Schools* was published in 1977. It recommended that grouping of schools under one governing body should be abolished and that there should be equal representation on every school's governing body of LEA, parents, staff and community. It also advocated extensions of their responsibility and emphasised the need for governors' training.

## THE 1980 ACT

The outcome was the Education Act 1980 which went a little way to meeting the Taylor Committee's recommendations. It required all schools to have at least two directly-elected parents and one or two teacher governors, plus the Head ex-officio if he or she wished to be a governor. LEAs could still retain a majority if they wished. The Act also did not take on board the recommendations for changes in functions for the governing body. New regulations, however, The Education (School Governing Bodies) Regulations 1981, gave the proceedings of the governing bodies some statutory coherence.

## THE 1986 ACT

Finally the Education (No.2) Act 1986 transformed both the composition and responsibilities of governing bodies. It gives governors more specific duties than hitherto and ensures that the distribution of functions between LEA, Governors and Head is more uniform than previously. It has far-reaching implications for the conduct of county, voluntary and maintained special schools, and some of its provisions touch not only schools in England and Wales, but also Northern Ireland, Scotland and independent schools.

Sir Keith Joseph, the then Secretary of State and main begetter of the act, said at the outset that the aim was to re-establish school governing bodies as a force for good in the life of individual schools and the communities they serve. Sir Keith was of the view that while significant advances had taken place in the government of schools following the 1980 Act, there were still obstacles that stood in the way of a more self-confident role for governing bodies. First was the insufficient account taken of parents' interests, second was the domination of the LEA, and third was the haphazard way in which governing bodies' powers had developed.

When the Act received Royal Assent, the Rt.Hon.Kenneth Baker, Education Secretary, welcomed it saying that "it provided new opportunities for parents, teachers, LEAs and others to work more effectively together in providing the best possible education for our children". The marked use of the word "reasonable" throughout the Act signifies how much good faith is placed in the partnership ideal.

## GERBIL (THE GREAT EDUCATION REFORM BILL)

In November 1987 the Secretary of State published a Bill which will increase even further governing bodies' powers. They will have extra powers over finance, admission of pupils, appointment of Heads, and even the legal status of the school. Those who become governors in the future will have to devote a substantial amount of time and thought to their responsibilities. On the other hand the powers to influence the curriculum of the school laid down in the 1986 Act will be circumscribed by new requirements for a National Curriculum.

# LEGAL AND ADMINISTRATIVE BACKGROUND

The education system is regulated by various Education Acts. From these flow regulations (Statutory Instruments) which usually deal with detailed appreciation of the law. Circulars of guidance and Administrative Memoranda are also issued by the Department of Education and Science to explain the regulations. These in themselves do not have the force of law.

## THE SECRETARY OF STATE

The Secretary of State for Education and Science has a principal duty to promote the education of the people of England and Wales, but the Secretary of State for Wales has identical powers and responsibilities as regards schools. In Northern Ireland the Secretary of State has a wide range of powers to ensure the adequate and efficient provision of education.

## THE DEPARTMENT OF EDUCATION AND SCIENCE

The Department of Education and Science (DES) supervises the national policy and is divided into various branches each headed by an Under Secretary.

## LOCAL EDUCATION AUTHORITIES

Local Education Authorities (LEAs) are those local councils which have been given the task of administering education. The full council forms the Local Education Authority, but they are required under the 1944 Act to have one or more Education Committees. LEAs have many duties (things which they must do) and powers (things which they may do) but the general duty is to contribute towards "the spiritual, moral, mental and physical development of the community" by ensuring that efficient education is available in their areas (s.7 Education Act 1944).

## THE INSPECTION OF SCHOOLS

The Secretary of State has the power to inspect educational establishments under s.77 of the 1944 Act and has Her Majesty's Inspectors (HMIs) to undertake the task. The inspection of independent schools is covered in s.70 of the 1944 Act.

HMIs have a degree of independence from the DES as they are appointed by the Crown. While the headquarters are within the DES most HMIs work at regional level, so that local authorities get to know general and specialist inspectors quite well.

Governors are most likely to come into contact with HMIs when their school is formally inspected. HMIs will normally report orally to a governors' meeting and this will be followed by a written report. In 1982 the Secretary of State decided to publish the reports and these are available from the DES. The Secretary of State can require LEAs and Governing Bodies to respond to the reports, usually giving a three-month deadline.

# TYPES OF SCHOOLS

Schools in England and Wales which are not independent schools must be in at least one of the following categories:

1. County school maintained by the LEA.
2. Special schools maintained by the LEA.
3. Voluntary aided schools maintained by the LEA.
4. Voluntary controlled schools maintained by the LEA.
5. Special agreement schools maintained by the LEA.
6. Hospital schools.
7. Grant maintained schools.
8. City Technology Colleges.

The categories in Northern Ireland are:

1. Controlled schools.
2. Voluntary schools.
3. Controlled integrated schools.

## COUNTY SCHOOLS

These are schools in England and Wales wholly maintained by Local Education Authorities. Primary schools take children at the age of five, or slightly earlier at the discretion of the LEA. At the secondary stage, usually commencing at age 11 or 12, there is a plethora of different types (comprehensive, grammar, secondary modern, upper, high, middle, sixth form college, tertiary).

A middle school will be deemed to be a primary or secondary school according to whether the age range of pupils below the age of 11 is greater than that of pupils above 11. When they are the same, the Secretary of State may determine the designation (Education (Middle Schools) Regulations 1980).

## VOLUNTARY SCHOOLS

All voluntary schools have been established by voluntary bodies usually, but not necessarily, Church bodies. Some 95% are Church of England or Roman Catholic Schools. Both these Churches are organised in dioceses and have diocesan education organisations. In the case of the Church of England there are Diocesan Education Committees (established by the Diocesan Education Committee Measure passed by Parliament) and in the case of the Roman Catholic Church, Diocesan Schools or Education Commissions.

### Voluntary Aided Schools

A voluntary aided school is one that is maintained by the LEA but which was not established by the LEA. The voluntary body owns the school and the governors must be able and willing to provide 15% of the cost of improving or enlarging the school to bring it up to the required standard or, if it is a new school, 15% of the school building. The governors are responsible for the external repairs of the school building with an 85% grant from the DES. Running costs, including maintenance of playing fields, are the responsibility of the LEA.

There will be a trust deed, and *foundation governors* will be appointed to ensure that the conduct of the school conforms to the terms of the trust deed. The foundation governors form a majority on the governing body.

Teachers in aided schools are employed by the governors, but are paid by the LEA. However, s.80 of the Employment Protection (Consolidation) Act 1978 provides that where a teacher is dismissed by the governors the LEA is regarded as the employer for the purposes of any appeal against unfair dismissal.

Religious education is under the control of the governors. If the governors of an aided school are no longer able or willing to provide 15% of the cost of external repairs, then they have a duty to apply to the Secretary of State to become a controlled school (s.15 1944 Act). If the governors decide to discontinue the voluntary school they must give two years' notice (s.14 1944 Act) to the Secretary of State for Education and Science.

## Voluntary Controlled Schools

Controlled schools are also voluntary schools and the voluntary body owns the school. However, it is a school where the governors are unable or unwilling to find the 15% proportion of the cost of improving the school (s.15 of the 1944 Act). As with aided schools foundation governors, will be appointed. Teachers are appointed by the LEA following the procedures of the 1986 Act (see Chapter 10).

Religious education must be in accordance with the "Agreed Syllabus" but parents can request for their children denominational instruction for not more than two periods of the week (s.27(6) 1944 Act).

## Special Agreement Schools

These owe their existence to pre-1944 agreements between the Government and voluntary bodies. Since the 1986 Act new ones can be set up but special agreement schools can become aided schools.

Capital expenditure on the buildings is met by the voluntary body with a grant of not more than 85% from the DES as for aided schools.

The provision for religious education must be in accordance with the trust deed, but is mainly in line with aided schools.

Following the 1986 Act the teaching staff is appointed in the same way as in a controlled school, except for reserved teachers of denominational religious education. Here, the numbers of reserved teachers who can be employed must be in accordance with the original agreement.

Church of England special agreement schools can receive financial assistance under the Church Schools (Assistance by Church Commissioners) Measure 1958.

## HOSPITAL SCHOOLS

Hospital authorities are empowered to arran᷃ ᷃ with LEAs for the use of hospital premises as special schools (National Health Service Act 1946).

## GRANT MAINTAINED SCHOOLS

The arrangement for the establishment, maintenance and discontinuance of grant main-tained schools are laid out in Chapter IV of the 1987 Bill. These are in some considerable detail to which there will be further additions via subsequent regulations. In addition the DES will publish circulars of guidance in due course. Below is an outline of the provisions.

## Approval for Applications

Governing bodies of county or voluntary secondary schools and primary schools with more than 300 pupils may apply for grant maintained status having obtained the approval of a simple majority of the parents of pupils at the school who vote in a secret postal ballot. This ballot will be paid for wholly or in part by the Secretary of State. Governing bodies will be obliged to hold a ballot, even if not in favour of it, if they receive a written request to hold such a ballot from a number of parents of pupils at the school equal to at least 20% of the number of registered pupils at the school.

## Application Proposals

If the governors are given the go-ahead they have six months in which to publish proposals for the acquisition of grant maintained status. The details to be contained in the proposal are specified in the Bill and will undoubtedly be made clearer in a subsequent DES circular. A two month objection period is allowed for before the Secretary of State will consider the proposals. He may reject, approve, or modify the proposals after consultation with the governing body.

If the application coincides with proposals for a re-organisation or closure of the school made under s.12 or s.13 of the 1980 Act, the Secretary of State will consider both proposals together, but will decide on the grant maintained application first. If grant maintained status is approved the Secretary of State will make the Instrument and Articles of Government.

## Composition of the Governing Body

The governing body will consist of:
  (a) five elected parent governors
  (b) one or two elected teacher governors
  (c) the Head
  (d) a number of "first" (in the case of ex-county schools) or "foundation" (in the case of ex-voluntary schools) governors to outnumber the other governors. At least two of these first or foundation governors must be parents of registered pupils at the time they take office.
The Secretary of State also has the power to appoint up to two additional governors if the governing body appears to him to be failing its responsibilities.

## Articles of Government

The Articles will set out the functions of the Secretary of State and governing body including admission policies, implementation of the National Curriculum and procedures for dealing with parents' complaints concerning admissions, exclusions and the curriculum.

## Transfer

On the due date the premises will transfer from the former maintaining authority to the governing body, and the staff employed at the school will also transfer, unless any of them decided not to.

## Character of the School

The school must retain the same character after the change as before and will not be able to charge fees. A change of character could be applied for but will be subject to statutory proposals, objection periods and determination by the Secretary of State.

## Financial Arrangements

The Secretary of State will pay an annual maintenance grant in respect of running costs. He will also be empowered to pay a 100 per cent grant on capital expenditure and may also provide special purpose grants. Details of these will be covered in future regulations.

## Services by LEAs

The LEA which formerly maintained the school will still have the power to provide certain services (eg school transport, clothing, board and lodging). In so doing it must treat pupils at a grant maintained school no less favourably than at schools maintained by them.

## Discontinuance

If governing bodies wish to discontinue the school as a grant maintained school, they will be required to publish proposals. Procedures for objection and determination will be laid down.

# CITY TECHNOLOGY COLLEGES

The Education Reform Bill 1987 in Chapter 5 allows the Secretary of State to enter into agreements with any persons wishing to set up a City Technology College (CTC) which:
  (a) is in an urban area
  (b) provides education free of charge for pupils of different abilities aged 11-19 from the local community, and
  (c) has a broad curriculum with an emphasis on science and technology.
  The chapter also provides for long-term funding arrangements to be agreed between the Secretary of State and the colleges, covering capital and recurrent costs. Running costs will be met by the Secretary of State in line with maintained schools on a per capita basis. However, the promoters must meet the capital costs. The Education (Grants) (City Technology Colleges) Regulations 1987 (SI 1987 No. 1138) enable the Secretary of State to pay grants to persons other than LEAs to maintain or alter CTCs.
  The colleges' governing bodies will also be bound to run the colleges in line with other conditions and requirements laid down by the Secretary of State. Other than this they will be treated as independent schools.

# NORTHERN IRELAND SCHOOLS

Public education in Northern Ireland is administered by five local Education and Library Boards. They manage the controlled schools and are responsible for the maintenance of most voluntary schools.

## Controlled Schools

These schools are controlled by the five local Education and Library Boards which must make provision for the appointment of a board of governors for the management of each school. Two or more controlled primary schools can be grouped under one board of governors, if the Education and Library Board approves.

## Voluntary Schools

These are grant-aided schools with governing bodies including trustees of the foundations which set them up.

## Controlled Integrated Schools

These are schools established under the Education (Northern Ireland) Act 1978. The aim is to attract pupils of different religious backgrounds and traditions. Each integrated school has a management committee.

# INDEPENDENT SCHOOLS

Schools which are not maintained by the LEA or do not receive grants from the Secretary of State are accountable to the governors or proprietors. They are subject to a certain amount of state control in that Part III of the Education Act 1944 is concerned with them. Independent schools are required to be registered with the DES (s.70 of the 1944 Act confirmed in s.34 of the Education Act 1980), and s.71 provides that the Secretary of State can serve notices of complaint on independent schools after registration if:

(a) the premises become unsuitable or
(b) the teaching standards fall below that suitable for pupils (having regard to their age and sex) or
(c) if the proprietor or any teacher is unsuitable to be the proprietor or teacher. Appeals against the notice of complaint can be made by the school to the Independent Schools' Tribunal (s.72).

Some LEAs pay for pupils to attend independent schools but are not obliged to do so. Some independent schools also take pupils on the *assisted places scheme* (see page 9).

## Registration of Independent Schools

Governors of independent schools must ensure that the school is registered under s.70 of the 1944 Act. The schools will then be on the register kept by the Registrar of Independent Schools. S.34 of the 1980 Act brought all ex-Direct Grant schools and schools previously not registered into the registration requirements.

The proprietors must furnish the Registrar with such particulars relating to the school as may be required. The Education (Particulars of Independent Schools) Regulations 1982 (SI 1982 No.1730) contain details of applications for registration, the making of annual returns, reporting of dismissals of staff on the grounds of misconduct and removal of schools from the register.

## Notice of Complaint

If the Secretary of State finds that the school premises are unsuitable, or the accommodation inadequate, or the instruction provided is inefficient and unsuitable, or that the proprietor or any employee is not a proper person to be a proprietor or teacher at the school, he will serve a notice of complaint specifying necessary measures to be taken and the time allowed for taking the appropriate measures (s.71 of the 1944 Act). The complaint could be referred to the Independent Schools Tribunal, to which the person(s) complained of can also appeal (s.72 of the 1944 Act).

## Striking Off

The Secretary of State or Independent Schools Tribunal can order that a school should be struck off the Register and any breach of the disqualification could lead to a fine or imprisonment (s.73). S.75 of the 1944 Act governs the proceedings of the Tribunal.

## Payment for Places at Independent Schools by Local Authorities

LEAs can make arrangements for the provision of education at non-maintained schools under s.6 Education (Miscellaneous Provisions) Act 1953 or for the assistance with fees at such schools under regulations made under the 1944 Act. S.8 of the 1980 Act requires LEAs to publish details of their arrangements and the criteria used to determine those eligible to receive assistance.

## Independent Schools and Parents

The relationship between governors or proprietors of independent schools and parents is affected more by the law of contract than it is by detailed statutory requirements.

Both parent and school usually enter into legal agreements which give both parties significant powers and rights, directly enforceable by each other. A parent cannot interfere in the running of the school, but nevertheless has a right to expect that the information given about the school and any inducements that may have been contained in the prospectus are fulfilled. Parents would have a claim against the school if they could prove that they were not getting what was promised. If they cannot prove justification, then if they withdrew their children they would be liable for the appropriate fees.

Parents of children in an independent school could not, for example, object to particular subjects on offer, or particular punishments (so long as they are legal ones) if they knew of these at the time of entering into the contract. Where a contract is silent on a particular point then reasonable decisions made by the school and common practice in the school would prevail.

## HOME TUITION

S.56 of the 1944 Act allows primary and secondary education to be provided "otherwise than at school". This chapter empowers parents to arrange for their children to be fully educated out of school, but they must prove to the satisfaction of Inspectors that suitable and efficient education according to the age and aptitude of the child is being given. Home tuition may also be provided by the LEA either by reason of the handicap or illness of the child or because the child has been excluded from school.

# The Government of Schools

## 2

## INSTRUMENT AND ARTICLES OF GOVERNMENT

The *Instrument of Government* is the term used for the legal order to provide for the constitution of a governing body. The Education (No.2) Act 1986 provides for every LEA to make new instruments for county, voluntary and maintained special schools.

Instruments specify the composition of the governing body, the terms of office, the conduct of meetings and may include other matters. The DES has published Model Instruments for different types of schools. There are no Model Instruments for aided and special agreement schools as the composition of their governing bodies has not changed.

The *Articles of Government* define the powers, duties and responsibilities of the governing body. As with the Instrument of Government, the 1986 Act stipulates that LEAs must make new Articles which will take effect from 1.9.88 for all county and maintained special schools and 1.9.89 for voluntary schools. The DES has produced a number of different Model Articles varying according to type of school.

These two documents, forming the main legal and working documents of the governing body, must incorporate all the necessary statutory provisions. DES Circular 7/87, *Education (No.2) Act: Further Guidance*, advises LEAs to ensure that the documents are comprehensive and straightforward. LEAs are also advised to avoid significant rephrasing of the Model Instruments and Articles which the DES has published since these draw heavily on the wording of the Act. Each school is entitled to its own Instruments and Articles but LEAs may provide block Instruments and Articles so long as they indicate clearly the name of the school to which each applies and include any distinctive provisions for individual schools.

LEAs are required under s.2 of the Act to consult the governing body and the Head of each school before producing new Instruments and Articles. In the case of *voluntary schools* the LEA must obtain the agreement of the governing body to the proposed terms, and must have regard to how the school has been conducted previously.

### ALTERATIONS

If governing bodies of any type of school propose alterations to the Instruments and Articles for their schools, the LEA has a duty to consider these (s.2(3)).

### VARIATION OF A TRUST DEED

It is possible that a proposed Instrument may be inconsistent with a trust deed relating to a school. In this case the Secretary of State has the power to modify the trust deed as appears to him to be just and expedient. The initiative rests with the school.

## LACK OF AGREEMENT

If the governors of voluntary schools and the LEA cannot agree over proposed terms, either party can refer the dispute to the Secretary of State, who will give such directions as he sees fit.

In the case of county and maintained special schools, if they feel that the LEA has not given due consideration or has in any way unreasonably rejected their proposals, it might be possible for them to refer the matter to the Secretary of State under provisions of the 1944 Act (see Chapter 14).

## EFFECT OF CHANGES IN SCHOOLS' CIRCUMSTANCES

The composition of a governing body depends on the number of pupils on roll in the case of county, controlled and maintained special schools (s.3 1986 Act). However, frequent changes in composition are prevented by the provision of s.11. The occasions on which adjustments can be made are limited to certain "relevant events". Generally this means a review every four years, or when a proposal for an increase in intake is implemented, or there is a change of site. Such events set a new baseline for subsequent four-year reviews.

The procedures for variation of the instrument are laid down in ss. 13 and 14 and are incorporated in paragraphs 2(3) (or for controlled schools 2(5)), 3 and 4 of the Schedule to the Model Instruments. The gist of these is contained in the following paragraphs.

### Change of Circumstance

S.13 sets the ground rules for variation of the Instrument when schools change their size or alter their nature in some way, eg "amalgamate". The LEA can either vary the Instrument or make a new one. But any changes in the Instrument in respect of the change in pupil numbers shall not be made until the fourth-year review is made.

### Reduction in Numbers of the Governing Body

S.14 resolves the problem of what to do if there is a need to reduce the governing body in a particular category of governors. Firstly, one or more in that category could resign; secondly, the ones selected to cease to hold office shall be selected in order of seniority, ie the longest serving governor will be the first to go, and so on. If two or more are equal in seniority then it shall be achieved by drawing lots.

This does not apply to foundation governors. In their case the Instrument must make provision for the procedure to be adopted. No particular procedure is set out in the Model Instrument.

## CONTENT OF INSTRUMENTS OF GOVERNMENT

Sections 1(5) and 8(9) and (10) allow the inclusion in Instruments of other matter not contained in the Act or in additions. The additions in the Model Instrument are drawn from the Education (School Government) Regulations 1987, to which any additions made by governors or LEAs would be subject. In general the Instrument should be a clear guide to the composition, meetings and proceedings of governors.

## COPIES TO ALL GOVERNORS AND TEACHERS

All members of the governing body and every teacher at the school must be given (free of charge) a copy of the Instruments and Articles for their school.

# ELIGIBILITY TO BE A GOVERNOR (S.15 1986 Act)

1. Where a school has two headteachers, for whatever reason, they shall both be governors unless either chooses not to be.
2. Any person qualified for election or appointment as a governor in a particular category shall not be disqualified from being elected or appointed as a governor of that school in any other category.
3. No one can hold more than one governorship of the same school at the same time.
4. No one may be qualified to be a governor unless aged eighteen or over at the date of election or appointment.

This section does not rule out pupil governors but does make it difficult as very few would qualify. Although the Secretary of State did not believe it appropriate for pupils to be governors of the schools they attend, he did consider it beneficial for pupils to become involved in the work of governing bodies and governors should, he feels, consider whether and how such involvement could be developed.

## TENURE OF OFFICE (S.8)

Governors other than ex-officio governors hold office for a four-year term, but can be re-elected or re-appointed for further terms. Parent governors whose child leaves the school may, therefore, complete their term of office. Teacher governors, however, must relinquish their governorships when they leave the school.

Governors who replace others during a term of office will serve for a new four-year term.

## REMOVAL FROM OFFICE (S.8(4) and (5))

Governors may resign or, in the case of appointed (not elected or co-opted) governors, be removed from office early by those who appointed them.

# EDUCATION (SCHOOL GOVERNMENT) REGULATIONS 1987

## DISQUALIFICATION

The disqualification provisions below (r.5 8 and 15) are exhaustive, and consequently no other categories can be introduced, eg in Instruments of Government.

1. Anyone holding more than four governorships of schools will be disqualified from governorship of all those schools but without prejudice to being re-elected as a governor of one to four schools.
2. An ex-officio member who holds more than four ex-officio memberships can designate which ones to continue with up to four.
3. A person adjudged bankrupt is disqualified until discharged from bankruptcy.

4. A person convicted of a crime and sentenced to a period of three months or more imprisonment within five years before or since his or her appointment or election as a governor is disqualified; similarly a person convicted under s.40 of the Local Government (Miscellaneous Provisions) Act 1982 (a trespasser on school premises who has caused a disturbance) is disqualified.

5. Any governor (other than an ex-officio or temporary governor) who, without the consent of the governing body concerned, fails to attend meetings for twelve months is disqualified, but may be reappointed or re-elected.

6. Teacher governors are disqualified from being governors when they cease to be teachers at the school.

7. Parent governors are *not* required to cease to hold office when their children leave the school.

## WRITTEN NOTICE

A Head who decides to exercise his or her right not to be a governor or who decides to revoke that right must give written notice to the Clerk. (r.16).

If a governor resigns or is removed written notice must be given to the Clerk (r.17).

## NOTIFICATION OF APPOINTMENTS AND VACANCIES (R.18)

The Clerk must give notice to the authority, body or persons by whom the vacancy falls to be filled when a member's term of office is about to expire, unless they have notified the Clerk of an appointment to the vacancy. The authority or other body must give the Clerk written notice of any appointment they make to the governing body specifying name and usual address of the person.

## DELEGATION OF FUNCTIONS

Governors may not delegate their functions except where given statutory authority (as in certain matters of finance and the appointment of staff). They can, however, ask one or more governors to consider a particular issue and report back. They must give full and proper consideration to that report so that any decision is that of the whole governing body. However, there are special arrangements for the Chairman or Vice-Chairman to act in an emergency (see below).

## POWER OF CHAIRMAN OR VICE-CHAIRMAN TO ACT IN CASES OF EMERGENCY

If the governing body as a whole is unable to act in an emergency and a delay is likely to affect adversely the school or a pupil, parent or employee at the school, then the Chairman (or Vice-Chairman if the Chairman cannot be contacted) has the power to discharge any of its functions. A delay means a period extending beyond the day preceding the earliest date on which it would be reasonably practicable for a meeting of the governing body to be held.

## POWER OF LOCAL EDUCATION AUTHORITY TO ACT ALONE (PART IV OF THE REGULATIONS)

The regulations give certain emergency powers to the LEA in circumstances where normally the LEA would have a duty to consult the governors.

### Exclusions of Pupils from School

Where a pupil has been excluded from school in circumstances where an opportunity to take a public examination would be lost, the LEA in desiring to direct the Head to reinstate the pupil would normally need to consult the governors. If the LEA is unable to contact the Chairman or Vice-Chairman and there is no time to call a governors' meeting, the LEA may direct the Head without consultation with the governors (r.28).

### Appointment of Teachers at County, Controlled, Special Agreement and Maintained Special Schools

Where an LEA has needed as a matter of urgency to redeploy a particular teacher in their employ, in accordance with s.38 of the 1986 Act, but is unable to contact the Chairman or Vice-Chairman of the receiving school, the LEA may proceed without consultation (r.29).

# POWER OF HEAD TO ACT IN MATTERS OF URGENCY

Under s.16 of the 1986 Act the Secretary of State can make regulations as to the circumstances where the LEA or Head can take steps as a matter of urgency without consulting the governors.

# BREAKDOWN IN RELATIONSHIPS

## DISPUTES

The determination of disputes is covered by s.67 of the 1944 Act.

If there is a dispute between the LEA and governors that cannot be settled between them the matter can be referred to the Secretary of State for his determination.

## UNREASONABLE BEHAVIOUR

The Secretary of State is empowered by s.68 of the 1944 Act to intervene if any person complains to him that a local authority or governing body of any county or voluntary school has acted, or is preparing to act, unreasonably. The Secretary of State can give such directions as appear to him to be expedient. It would be open to a governing body to complain about the unreasonable acts of the LEA and for parents to complain about unreasonable acts of the governing body. The LEA could complain about a governing body.

# FAILURE TO DISCHARGE DUTIES

Where, however, the LEA or governing body fails to discharge a statutory duty, the Secretary of State may make an order declaring the LEA or governors to be in default and to give such directions as he sees fit to ensure that they fulfil their duties (s.99 of the 1944 Act) (See also Chapter 5).

# The Composition of Governing Bodies

**3**

## MAINTAINED SCHOOLS
### COUNTY, CONTROLLED AND MAINTAINED SPECIAL SCHOOLS

The composition of governing bodies for these schools is covered by s.3 of the Education (No.2) Act 1986 and is set out in the chart below:

| Number of Pupils | Type and Number of Governors | | | | | |
|---|---|---|---|---|---|---|
| | Parents | LEA | Head | Teachers | Co-opted* | TOTAL |
| Up to 99 | 2 | 2 | 1 | 1 | 3 (2/1)* | 9 |
| 100-299 | 3 | 3 | 1 | 1 | 4 (3/1)* | 12 |
| 300-599 | 4 | 4 | 1 | 2 | 5 (4/1)* | 16 |
| 600 or more | 5 | 5 | 1 | 2 | 6 (4/2)* | 19 |

*or, for controlled schools: foundation/co-opted.

The Act also allows the Instrument of Government to provide that the formula for the 300–599 school could be used for 600+ schools, thus reducing the number of governors in these schools to 16.

The new governing bodies must be in place by 1.9.88 for all county and maintained special schools. Foundation governors for controlled schools must be at least one fifth of the total governing body.

The composition reflects the numbers on roll as calculated from when the Instrument is made, and in the case of new or enlarged schools the projected roll at the end of the build-up period.

### COMPOSITION OF GOVERNING BODIES FOR AIDED AND SPECIAL AGREEMENT SCHOOLS (S.4 OF THE 1986 ACT)

There is no fixed limit for governing bodies of these schools, but they must include:
   (a) at least one governor appointed by the LEA
   (b) in the case of primary schools serving an area in which there is a minor authority (see page 21), at least one governor appointed by that authority
   (c) foundation governors

(d) at least one parent governor

(e) at least one teacher governor (in schools with less than 300 registered pupils) or at least two teachers in schools over 300

(f) the Head (unless he or she chooses not to be a governor).

The number of foundation governors must outnumber the other governors by *two* if the governing body consists of eighteen or fewer, or *three* if there are more than eighteen. At least one foundation governor must be a parent at the time of the appointment. For the purposes of calculating the required number of foundation governors, the Head should be counted as a governor, even if choosing not to be one. Governors other than those required by this section can also be appointed.

All voluntary schools' governing bodies must conform to this composition by September 1989.

## NEW SCHOOLS AND TEMPORARY GOVERNING BODIES

Temporary governing bodies for new schools will be constituted as above for the relevant type of school.

## NURSERY SCHOOLS

The 1986 Act makes no provisions for governance of nursery schools. However, LEAs are free to make local arrangements.

## COMMUNITY SCHOOLS

The designation "community school" does not affect the legal status. LEAs may, however, assign functions relating to non-school activities to a body identical in membership with the governing body. This means that the governors could include "community issues" on their agenda. It would also be possible for additional members to take part in governing bodies for the purpose of discussing the non-school activities, but they would be "observers" when school business was under discussion.

## REVIEW OF THE COMPOSITION OF GOVERNING BODIES OF COUNTY, CONTROLLED AND MAINTAINED SPECIAL SCHOOLS

S.11 of the 1986 Act limits the occasions on which subsequent adjustments must be considered. Generally, consideration is to be given every four years and when some proposal providing for an increase in the number of pupils is implemented. This will set a new baseline for subsequent four-year reviews. The manner in which these adjustments are to be made is set out in ss.13 and 14 of the Act (See Chapter 2).

# NEW SCHOOLS

## TEMPORARY GOVERNING BODIES

S.12 and schedule 2 of the Education (No.2) Act 1986 contain new requirements for the establishment of temporary governing bodies for new county, voluntary and maintained special schools. The requirements are designed to enable the various interests represented to take part in important decisions prior to the opening.

If the school in question is a controlled or aided school the LEA must consult the promoters about whether to form a temporary governing body before the Secretary of State's approval is given (s.12(5) and (6)). If there is a disagreement either side could refer the dispute to the Secretary of State.

### Definition of a New School

It is one which is required to have a temporary governing body or one where proposals for new maintained schools have been published under s.12(4).

### Where a Temporary Governing Body is required

When the Secretary of State has approved an LEA proposal for a new county school or for the maintenance of a school it has not maintained previously, the LEA must arrange for the constitution of a temporary governing body, pending the constitution of its eventual governing body (s.12(1) and (2)).

### New Special Schools

If the school is a new special school the temporary governing body must be constituted at least one year before pupils are expected to be admitted *or* on the day on which the resolution to establish the school is passed (s.12 (3)).

The LEA is also enabled to make arrangements for a temporary governing body in anticipation of the Secretary of State's approval (s.12 (4)).

### Function of Temporary Governing Bodies

The functions of temporary governing bodies, LEAs and Heads in relation to new schools are set out in Part III of schedule 2 to the 1986 Act. In the main the functions are the same as those of full governing bodies, with some alterations, because the school is not yet in operation. In the main they will determine any matters relating to the conduct of the school that need to be determined before a governing body is constituted. Guidance is provided in Circular 7/87 *Education (No.2) Act 1986: Further Guidance Annex 1.*

## INDEPENDENT SCHOOLS

The composition will either be set out in a trust deed or by a resolution of the proprietor or directors where the independent school is privately owned or is a company.

## ELECTIONS AND APPOINTMENTS TO GOVERNING BODIES

Some governors are elected (normally parent and teacher governors) some are appointed (usually LEA and representative governors), some are co-opted (eg foundation governors, or persons with local business community connections) and some are ex-officio (eg the Head or Diocesan Education Officer). Representative governors are appointed to represent minor authorities or voluntary bodies or, in the case of hospitals schools, the health authority.

## ELECTION OF PARENT AND TEACHER GOVERNORS

The LEA (or governing body of an aided school) must make all the necessary arrangements for parent and teacher governors, and must determine who is a parent of a registered pupil and who is a teacher at the school. They may also make provision as to qualifying dates if they so wish (s.15(3) of the 1986 Act).

### Definition of a Parent

A parent is defined in s.114 of the 1944 Act as including a guardian and every person who has the actual custody of the child. It is thus possible for a child to have more than two parents eligible to participate in an election. The responsible authority does not have to track down every person who might qualify but s.15 (6) of the 1986 Act makes it clear that the authority cannot rule ineligible anyone known to them to be a "parent".

### Disqualification

The responsible authority should ensure that the disqualification categories (see Chapter 2) are made known to anyone thinking of standing for election.

### No Age Limit

A maximum age limit for parent governors is ruled out by s.15 (6).

## PRE-ELECTION PUBLICITY

The governors' annual reports to parents are required to provide any available information about the arrangements for the next election of parent governors (s.30(2)(g)). The responsible authority must also give publicity to the election process. This is commonly done by letter through "pupil post". The letter should be translated into other languages where a substantial number of parents has a language other than English as their mother tongue.

## CONDUCT OF THE ELECTION

The responsible authority has the duty to make the arrangements. DES circular No. 7/87, Annex 9 paragraphs 18-25, offers detailed guidance about nominations and the conduct of the election. The responsible authorities should decide how nominations are to be made, eg whether a proposer and seconder are required or a larger number of sponsors, and indicate whether those nominated must signify their willingness to stand. All should be parents of registered pupils. Responsible authorities are also recommended to appoint a presiding or returning officer who could be the Chairman or Head or Clerk to the governors. They must also select the electoral method which might be the first past the post or proportional representation. If the latter is chosen the presiding or returning officer should be familiar with the intricacies of the system. The responsible authority must also determine whether a parent is to have one vote per child per vacancy or only one per vacancy. The ballot paper should list names of candidates either in alphabetical order or at random, and it could include a personal statement from each candidate. Each parent must be provided with one ballot paper. Clear instructions on voting should be given. The ballot must be secret.

## Secret Ballot

S.15 (4) of the 1986 Act provides that the election must be made by secret ballot. A requirement that the ballot paper be signed by the voter is not consistent with secrecy, and the DES circular advises the use of a double envelope system (Annex 8 paragraph 25) where the ballot paper is sealed in an inner unmarked envelope which is then sealed in an outer envelope. This is signed on the back by the voter. The presiding officer would check the outer envelope for entitlement to vote and put the unmarked envelope into the ballot box.

## Return of Ballot Papers

In the case of parent governor elections every person entitled to vote must have the opportunity to do so by post or, if he or she prefers, to return the ballot paper via a pupil at the school (s.15 (5)).

It is up to the responsible authority to devise how this requirement is to be combined with personal and proxy voting (if any is to be allowed). The circular offers some guidance in Annex 8, paragraphs 25-29.

## Postal Votes

There is no requirement for postal votes though they are not excluded. If postal votes are not allowed the case for proxy voting is strengthened (paragraph 34).

## The Count

The count should be conducted by the returning officer at a time and place determined by the responsible authority. This officer should be responsible for deciding the validity of dubious or spoilt ballot papers but should be able to refer to a nominee of the responsible authority in difficult cases (paragraph 30).

The responsible authority should make clear, before the election, the method for deciding an election in the event of a tie. The votes should first be re-counted. After that other methods must be considered such as drawing lots, tossing a coin or choosing the candidate with the youngest child (paragraph 31).

The responsible authority does not have the power to impose any requirement as to the minimum number of votes required to be cast for a candidate to be elected (s.15 (3) of the 1986 Act).

## POST ELECTION

The result of the election should be notified by the responsible authority to all parents, the remainder of the governors and the LEA. The ballot papers should be retained for a period, say six months, and in order to monitor participation the number of ballot papers issued and returned should be noted (paragraphs 22 and 33).

The election procedures should be reviewed from time to time.

## TEACHER GOVERNOR ELECTIONS (PARAGRAPH 34)

The guidance given for parent governor elections is generally valid for teacher governor elections too. It is recommended that responsible authorities should consult teacher associations at local level on their proposed election arrangements.

The Head can participate as a candidate, though if elected he may not also be an ex-officio governor (s.15(10)). The Head may vote in elections for teacher governors as a teacher at the school.

## Temporary, Part-time and Supply Teachers

The responsible authority must make their eligibility clear. Normally supply teachers should be excluded as they are unlikely to be teachers *at* the school, but part-timers should be included.

# APPOINTMENT OF GOVERNORS

## LEA GOVERNORS

The LEA is free to choose its representatives as it thinks fit. The Secretary of State has expressed the hope that they would be chosen on the basis of the strengths they can contribute to the effective discharge of the governing body's function (paragraph 5.3.6 Circular 7/87).

## MINOR AUTHORITY GOVERNORS (S.7 OF THE 1986 ACT)

When a county or controlled primary school serves an area in which there is a minor authority, the Instrument must provide for one governor to be appointed by the minor authority (a Parish Council as under s.114 of the 1944 Act). Where there is more than one minor authority in the area served by the school, the authorities are to act jointly in appointing a governor. The Secretary of State may make an appointment if they fail to agree. Minor authorities could also be represented via an LEA appointment or co-option.

The governor appointed by the minor authority takes the place of a co-opted governor.

## VOLUNTARY ORGANISATION APPOINTMENTS

Maintained special schools (other than those in hospitals) with fewer than 100 pupils shall have one governor appointed by an appropriate voluntary organisation, or jointly by two or more voluntary organisations, designated by the LEA. If there are more than 99 pupils, the Instrument shall provide for two governors to be appointed (s.7(3)).

If the LEA is satisfied that there is no appropriate voluntary organisation this requirement will not apply to the Instrument.

## HOSPITAL SPECIAL SCHOOLS

In the case of a maintained special school established in a hospital, the Instrument must provide for one governor to be appointed by the district health authority (s.7(2)).

## APPOINTMENT OF PARENT GOVERNORS AT COUNTY, CONTROLLED OR MAINTAINED SPECIAL SCHOOLS

Normally parent governors must be elected but there are occasions when they may simply be appointed:

(a) when the LEA decides that elections are not practicable for a maintained special
    school in a hospital school (s.5(3)). The LEA will wish to take into account the views
    of governors during the required consultation and any previous practice before the
    Instrument is made
(b) where insufficient parents stand for election as parent governors
(c) where provision is made in the Instrument and where the LEA concludes that parent
    governor elections are impracticable in a county, controlled or maintained special
    school (other than in a hospital) at which at least 50% of the pupils are boarders
    (including weekly boarders).

Unlike the position in (b) above such a decision must be taken on each occasion. LEAs
must take into account previous practice and any governors' views on this, both in framing
the initial Instrument and determining individual cases.

In the cases above the governors must appoint a person who is the parent of a registered
pupil at the school when it is reasonably practicable to do so, and where it is not, to appoint
a parent of one or more children of compulsory school age. They cannot on the other hand
appoint an elected member of the LEA, an employee of the authority or the governing
body of an aided school maintained by the LEA, or a co-opted member of any education
committee of the authority (s.5 (4)).

This section of the 1986 Act attempts to ensure that governing bodies are not "packed"
with employees or members of LEAs. Employees and members of LEAs who are also
parents may, of course, be elected by the parents, if they are otherwise eligible.

## CO-OPTED GOVERNORS

Governing bodies of county, controlled and maintained special schools are required by s.3
of the 1986 Act to co-opt other governors. The Instrument for county, controlled and
maintained special schools specifies that the governors in co-opting other governors must
have regard to the extent to which they and these other governors are members of the local
business community.

By virtue of s.15(2) governing bodies are not to be constrained by any direction of an
LEA or provision in the Instrument in their co-option of other governors. They should,
however, take note of their own strengths and appoint those who will add to the links with
the community the school serves. They could also use the opportunity to appoint representatives of non-teaching staff who no longer have the right to a seat on the governing body
under the new Act.

### No Vacancies

It is important to note that no place(s) on the governing body can be left vacant.

# FOUNDATION GOVERNORS

These are defined in s.114 of the 1944 Act as governors appointed to any voluntary school
otherwise than by an LEA or a minor authority for the purpose of securing that the

character of the school as a voluntary school is preserved and developed, and that the school is conducted in accordance with the provision of the trust deed.

Foundation governors may be appointed:

(a) by bodies to be specified under 2.15(7) in the Instrument, or

(b) by co-option by certain other governors

(c) ex-officio (s.15 (8)).

by the holder of an office named in the Instrument.

# Governing Body Proceedings

**4**

## CONDUCT OF BUSINESS

The conduct of governors' business both during and outside the actual governing body meetings is regulated more by good sense and good practice than law. Nevertheless there are statutory requirements — indeed many more than there used to be — following the 1980 and 1986 Education Acts. The Education (School Government) Regulations 1987, stemming from s.8 of the Education (No.2) Act 1986, cover the meetings and proceedings of governing bodies of all maintained schools. Instruments of Government may also make further provisions on these matters though by virtue of s.8 (10) of the 1986 Act, the Regulations take precedence. Except where otherwise stated the regulations apply to both governing bodies and temporary governing bodies of all maintained schools.

## MEETINGS (REGULATION 12)

### NUMBER OF MEETINGS

There must be at least one meeting per term. Temporary governing bodies may hold a meeting as often as necessary.

### CONVENING MEETINGS

The Clerk must give members at least seven days' notice — except in emergencies (r.19). The Clerk must also comply with any directions given by the governors at the previous meeting, or given by the Chairman (or Vice in his or her absence) so long as this is not inconsistent with the governing body's directions.

### QUORUM

For the smallest governing bodies this will be three. For larger governing bodies it will be one third (rounded up to a whole number) of the complete membership of the governing body where this results in a quorum greater than three (r.13(1)).

However, r.13 (2) provides that where an Instrument of Government specifies a greater number than that required by r.13(1) this figure will form the quorum of any meeting of the governing body, so long as it does not exceed two fifths (rounded up) of the complete membership of the governing body.

For certain purposes in county, controlled and maintained special schools the quorum must be three quarters (rounded up) of the governors concerned. These purposes are:

(a) making appointments of parent governors in accordance with any provision made under s.5 of the 1986 Act (See Chapter 3)
(b) co-opting governors (other than foundation governors) in accordance with s.3 of the 1986 Act or paragraph 2(1)(a) of schedule 2 of that Act
(c) co-opting temporary teacher governors in accordance with paragraph 8 of Schedule 2 of the Act.
If there is no quorum the meeting cannot be held.

## ELECTION OF CHAIRMAN AND VICE-CHAIRMAN (r.9)

A Chairman and Vice-Chairman must be elected at the first meeting of each school year (unless otherwise specified in the Instrument).

A casual vacancy may be filled at the next available meeting.

If the Chairman and Vice-Chairman are absent the members may elect one of their number to act as Chairman during their absence. No teacher or non-teacher employed at the school, or a pupil at the school, may be elected Chairman or Vice-Chairman of the governing body or of a meeting, but all other governors are eligible.

### Chairman and Vice-Chairman of Temporary Governing Bodies (r.10)

The regulations are the same as above but in addition, the Head of the new school, any temporary teacher, governors of the new school and anyone employed at the school other than as a teacher (or people who are likely to be employed other than as teachers) are ineligible.

## RIGHT OF HEAD TO ATTEND MEETINGS OF GOVERNORS (r.11)

A Head who is not a governor is entitled to attend any meeting of the governing body except in certain circumstances (See below, Withdrawal from Meetings).

## AGENDAS

The agenda is in the hands of the governing body which in practice usually means the Chairman or the Clerk to the governing body aided by the Head, although any member of the governing body could ask for items to be included. It is also usual for the LEA to ask for items to be included. Matters which regularly appear on the agendas of governing bodies include health and safety, school curriculum, financial report, annual report to parents, discipline, school closures, changes of staff.

## PROCEEDINGS AND MINUTES (r.14)

Questions put to a vote will be decided by a majority vote. The Chairman has a second or casting vote when voting is equal.

Minutes must be made and signed at the same or following meeting and the Chief Education Officer must be supplied with a copy on request. The minutes can be entered on loose leaves provided that the person signing them initials each leaf.

All those governors present must be recorded alongside the minutes (r.23).

## REVISION AND VARIATION OF RESOLUTIONS (AIDED AND SPECIAL AGREEMENT SCHOOLS)

A resolution to rescind or vary a resolution made at a previous meeting of the governing body of an aided or special agreement school cannot be proposed unless such a resolution is a specific item on the agenda (r.20(1)). This also applies to a controlled school if the Instrument of Government was made prior to 1.9.87 (r.20(2)).

## TERMINATION AND ADJOURNMENT OF MEETINGS

The proceedings of the governing body are not invalidated by any vacancies in their number nor by any defect in the election or appointment of any governor.

In the case of an aided or special agreement school:
  (a) if the governors resolve to terminate or adjourn a meeting during its course, the meeting will be terminated forthwith
  (b) if during the meeting the numbers fall below a quorum the meeting must terminate
  (c) in such cases any unfinished business must be held over to a special meeting convened as quickly as possible
  (d) if governors resolve to adjourn a meeting until a date and time specified in the resolution, the Clerk must endeavour to inform those members not present of the terms of the resolution (r.21).

## ATTENDANCE OF NON-GOVERNORS

The Head, if not a governor, and the Clerk attend as of right, but the governing body determines whether access to their meetings should be widened to include other persons.

DES Circular 7/87 *Education (No.2) Act 1986: Further Guidance* suggests that governors will wish to balance arguments in favour of openness against the need to maintain an atmosphere of informality and mutual trust. Access to meetings may be limited to certain classes such as education officers or members of staff, or senior pupils, or any other. Non-governors may only speak with the permission of the governors and may be asked to withdraw during certain items of business (r.22).

## ATTENDANCE OF THE CLERK

If necessary the governing body can meet without the Clerk. The Clerk's duties could be discharged by one of the governors without prejudice to that member's position as a governor (Article 21(4) or 22(4) for Controlled Schools).

# ACCESS TO MINUTES AND PAPERS OF MEETINGS OF GOVERNING BODIES

Agendas and minutes and any other papers considered at meetings must be made available for inspection at the school by anyone wishing to do so, although confidential material may be excluded (r.25). Governors must ensure that the Clerk and the Head are given proper instructions about what is confidential as they are likely to be the ones approached.

Confidential material is defined as material relating to:
  (a) named teachers or non-teachers employed at the school (or proposed to be employed)

(b) named pupils (or candidates for admission)

(c) any other matter which the governing body considers should be dealt with on a confidential basis because of its nature.

This provision concerning access to governing body papers does *not* extend to temporary governing bodies.

The minutes must be open to inspection by the LEA.

# REQUIREMENT FOR A SECOND MEETING OF THE GOVERNING BODY: AIDED AND SPECIAL AGREEMENT SCHOOLS

In the circumstances listed below a decision taken by governors of any aided or special agreement school cannot have effect unless confirmed at a second meeting of the governing body not less than 28 days after the first:

(a) when the decision would mean submission of proposals to establish or alter a voluntary school under s.13 of the Education Act 1980

(b) where any decision would be to serve a notice to discontinue the school under s.14(1) of the Education Act 1944

(c) where any decision would result in an application under s.15(4) of the 1944 Act (revocation of order whereby a school is an aided or special agreement school)

(d) where the decision would be to request the discontinuance of the school for which another one would be substituted or when a submission on that matter would be made to the Secretary of State, under s.16 of the 1944 Act

(e) where there might be a decision to agree to transfer the school to the LEA under schedule 2 of the 1944 Act.

# WITHDRAWAL FROM MEETINGS OF GOVERNORS

The withdrawal provisions contained in schedule 2 of the 1987 School Government Regulations are now exhaustive, except in respect of any pupil governors for whom further regulations could be made locally.

The only circumstances in which a governor must withdraw from a governors' meeting or disclose relevant information are as follows:

(a) if a member has a direct or indirect pecuniary interest in any proposed contract he or she must disclose the fact and take no part in the discussion of the matter and withdraw (unless the governing body otherwise allow) and not vote on any matter with respect to the contract. "*Indirect*" *interest* is explained in 2.(2) and (3) of schedule 2

(b) if a member is present when the appointment or promotion of himself or herself or a relative is under consideration he or she shall take no part in the discussion, and withdraw (unless the governing body allow otherwise) and not vote (paragraph 3)

(c) he or she must also do the same if a transfer, promotion or retirement is under consideration which would result in a vacant post for which he or she could be a candidate (paragraph 4)

(d) if a pupil or parent is present at a meeting where the admission of or disciplinary action against that pupil is being considered, the pupil or parent must take no part in the consideration, as in the cases above (paragraph 5)

(e) similarly with a member who has made allegations, or has been witness at an alleged accident which has given rise to diciplinary action against a pupil or teacher or non-teacher employed at the school, although the Head and CEO (or his or her representative) are not obliged to withdraw in this instance, but may not vote on the matter (paragraph 5(c))

(f) a member who has been concerned with disciplinary action against a pupil or employee at the school and is present at a meeting at which an appeal against that disciplinary action is under consideration, must take no part and must withdraw (paragraph 5(d))

(g) the same position applies where an employee is present at a meeting where disciplinary action against him or her is under consideration (paragraph 5(e))

(h) if a person who is a relative (other than a parent) is present at a meeting where the admission of or disciplinary action against that pupil or disciplinary action against another pupil involved in an incident with that pupil is under consideration, he or she must disclose the relationship as soon as possible after the meeting has begun (paragraph 6)

(i) if a person employed as a teacher or non-teacher at the school is present at a meeting of the governors at which his or her conduct or continued employment at the school or the appointment of a successor, is under discussion he or she must not (if a governor) vote on any question with respect to that matter and, whether or not a governor, must take no part in the discussion or consideration of the matter and must withdraw from the meeting during such consideration, unless the governing body decide otherwise (r.7).

Note that governing bodies can decide to waive some of these requirements and substitute other arrangements.


# DISPUTES ABOUT THE EXERCISE OF GOVERNORS' FUNCTIONS

Any disputes between LEAs and governing bodies can be referred to the Secretary of State who has a power under s.68 of the 1944 Act to prevent unreasonable exercise of functions by either the LEA or governing bodies of any county or voluntary school when he receives a complaint. He can give such directions as appear to him to be expedient. In the celebrated case of *The Secretary of State for Education and Science v Tameside Metropolitan Borough Council* 1977, Lord Diplock defined "unreasonableness" in public law as "conduct which no sensible authority acting with due appreciation of its responsibilities would have decided to adopt".

The Secretary of State is empowered by s.99 of the 1944 Act to direct LEAs or governing bodies as he considers expedient on receipt of a complaint (or otherwise) that they are in default of their duty.

In order to facilitate the Secretary of State's decision-making, he is empowered to require reports from governing bodies of maintained and voluntary schools (s.56 of the 1986 Act).

There is always a possibility of a recourse to the courts in appropriate cases, although such instances are rare. It is also possible for governing bodies to ask a High Court judge for a "declaratory judgment" which is a way of ascertaining the legal rights and duties of particular public bodies in specific situations. Once the law has been "declared" it must be observed.

# Governors and the School Curriculum

5

## THE NATIONAL CURRICULUM

The starting point for determining the curriculum in all schools (other than those independent ones which choose not to follow suit) will be the National Curriculum which was put before Parliament in the Education Reform Bill of 1987 (Part I, Chapter 1).

### Purpose of the National Curriculum

The Bill first of all states that the school curriculum in maintained schools must be balanced. It must also promote spiritual, moral, cultural, mental and physical development of the pupil at school, and prepare pupils for the opportunities, responsibilities and experience of adult life.

Governing bodies and Heads are given the duty to ensure that the curriculum of their school satisfies these requirements and that the National Curriculum is delivered. Governors must also ensure that the requirement for religious instruction in s.25 (2) of the Education Act 1944 is met.

### The Basic Curriculum

A "basic curriculum" for all pupils up to compulsory school leaving age is outlined in the Bill, comprising core and other foundation subjects. For each subject in these categories there will eventually be programmes of study and such attainment targets and assessment arrangements as the Secretary of State considers appropriate, at four "key stages" from the beginning to the end of compulsory schooling. The key stages are at around the age of 7; at 11; at 14 and at 16.

### CURRICULUM COUNCILS

To help him in this task the National Curriculum Council will be set up (with a parallel Curriculum Council for Wales), and the School Examinations and Assessment Council, each consisting of 10 to 15 members appointed by the Secretary of State.

### CORE AND FOUNDATION SUBJECTS

The *core* subjects in the Bill are Mathematics, English and Science (with Welsh in Welsh speaking schools). The other *foundation* subjects are History, Geography, Technology, Music, Art and Physical Education. In secondary schools (with pupils over 11 years old) a modern language will be added as specified in an order made of the Secretary of State (plus Welsh in non-Welsh speaking schools). The languages chosen are likely to be those of EC countries and others of major commercial importance. Religious Education is also included as a foundation subject.

A difference between *core* and *foundation* subjects is that the national programmes of study will be more detailed for the former. For some foundation subjects only guidelines might be issued to schools.

There is no requirement in the Bill that a school's timetable should include separate subject lessons in each core or foundation subject. There is also no particular amount of time that should be spent on the core and foundation subjects. Chapter 1 requires them to be taught for a "reasonable time in relation to the relevant key stage". In the standing committee the Minister suggested that they could be fitted into about 70% of the week.

The Secretary of State may amend these requirements, having first referred to the National Curriculum Council, or the Curriculum Council for Wales. There may also be subsequent orders specifying modifications for pupils in particular circumstances. Heads are also given the flexibility to treat individual students within a larger class differently if necessary.

## SPECIAL NEEDS

Statements of Special Education Need made under s.7 of the Education Act 1981 may also modify the National Curriculum requirements for that child and statemented children could be exempt from the National Curriculum (see Chapter 6).

## CURRICULUM DEVELOPMENT

Some schools will be allowed to carry out development work or experiments. For county, controlled and maintained special schools the LEA or Curriculum Council may apply to do so, with the agreement of the governors, to the Secretary of State. Where the Curriculum Council applies the agreement of the LEA is required. For aided, special agreement and grant maintained schools the governors may apply to the Secretary of State for a direction; or the Curriculum Council may do so with the governors' agreement.

## ATTAINMENT TARGETS

Some flexibility in the nature of attainment targets, programmes of study and assessment arrangements is envisaged. The Secretary of State is empowered to specify them as he considers appropriate.

## SYLLABUSES AND QUALIFICATIONS

The Bill provides that only relevant syllabuses and external qualifications approved by the Secretary of State can be offered in maintained schools to pupils of compulsory school age. There are also reserve powers to include qualifications for pupils up to the age of 19 in this category.

## PUBLICATION OF INFORMATION

The Secretary of State may make regulations requiring information to be provided either generally or in particular about a school's curriculum and assessment arrangements, and the results of assessment. These regulations will be subject to Parliamentary approval. Governors will have part of the responsibility for ensuring compliance with the requirement to provide this information, in addition to the requirements in other Acts, eg 1980 and 1986, to publish certain information.

## COMPLAINTS

LEAs, after consulting governing bodies of aided and special agreement schools, must make arrangements for considering and disposing of any complaints about the Authority's discharge of their functions regarding the National Curriculum, religious instruction, assessment or external qualifications. The Secretary of State will not entertain such a complaint under ss.68 or 99 of the 1944 Act unless the complaint has first been made and disposed of under the LEA's procedures (see also Chapters 2 and 5).

## GRANT MAINTAINED SCHOOLS AND THE NATIONAL CURRICULUM

All the provisions will apply to the new grant maintained schools (see Chapter 1 and below) except the clauses referring to publication of information and complaints.

## EXCEPTIONS

Nursery schools and nursery classes, and special schools in hospitals do not have to follow the requirements.

## INDEPENDENT SCHOOLS AND THE NATIONAL CURRICULUM

Although the Secretary of State does not intend the detailed provisions concerning the proposed National Curriculum, as set out in the Education Reform Bill 1987, to apply to independent schools he has made it clear that he expects existing independent schools to take notice of the requirements. The Secretary of State has also indicated new independent schools would be unlikely to obtain a licence from the Department of Education and Science unless they proposed to implement the National Curriculum.

In addition, the Secretary of State would expect Her Majesty's Inspectors to take full account of the National Curriculum policy when inspecting independent schools. When the Secretary of State studies the reports he will consider whether "efficient and suitable instruction" is being provided and in so doing will apply the substance of the National Curriculum before deciding on appropriate action.

# CURRICULUM POLICY

A school's curriculum, which was defined by Her Majesty's Inspectors in their document *A view of the Curriculum* as those school activities which "promote the intellectual, personal, social and physical development of pupils", includes both classroom and extra-curricular activities. There is still much left out of the National Curriculum on which LEAs and governing bodies are entitled, or have a duty, to have a policy, under the provisions of ss.17–20 of the Education (No.2) Act 1986. These provisions may be amended in due course but they stand for the moment and do not appear to conflict in any irreconcilable way with the provisions in the 1987 Education Reform Bill.

# THE DUTY OF THE LEA TO STATE CURRICULAR POLICY

Within the confines of the National Curriculum, when it is finally established, the LEA will still have a duty to determine and keep under review a secular curriculum policy for all the schools it maintains. It could, for example, include policies on health education, social education, work in the community, political education, field studies, residential experiences, work experience and many other matters that will aid or complement the implementation of the National Curriculum (s.17 1986 Act).

# THE DUTY OF THE GOVERNING BODY OF COUNTY, CONTROLLED AND MAINTAINED SPECIAL SCHOOLS TO STATE CURRICULAR POLICY

The governors, too, must have regard to the aims and particulars of the National Curriculum when carrying out duties to consider the LEA's policy and to consider the aims of the secular curriculum of their school (s.18 1986 Act). They, too, will be concerned with broader issues than the "basic curriculum" of the National Curriculum. They must consider how (if at all) the LEA's policy should be modified in relation to their school and then make a written statement of their conclusions (which they must keep up to date). As to the position of sex and political education, see below.

## Consultations Required

If the governors intend to modify the LEA's policy they must first consult the LEA. They must also consult the Head and *have regard to* any representations by members of the community and by the chief officer of police (when such representations are connected with that officer's responsibilities).

The phrase "have regard to" is not an empty one. Failure to give proper consideration to representations could be challenged in the courts or via the Ombudsman. The relationship with the Police is considered further below and in Chapter 8.

## Availability of Governors' Statement

The governors must give a copy of their statement on curricular policy to the Head, who must make it available at all reasonable times to persons wishing to inspect it.

## Governors' Policy Review

The governors may review their policy whenever they think fit. They *must* do so when there is a substantial change in the nature or size of the school (s.18(7)). When they have completed such a review they must hand fresh written statements to the Head and to the LEA.

## Relationships with the Police

Governing bodies of county, controlled and maintained special schools have a new duty, under s.18 of the 1986 Act, to have regard to any representations about curriculum matters made by the local chief officer of police (when such representations are connected with his or her responsibilities). Heads also have the same duty. Also, in their annual report to parents, governors must report what steps they have taken to strengthen links with the community, including the police. These requirements were made in order to strengthen the position of the police in seeking access to, and liaison with, schools for educational purposes, which had been under strain in some areas. There is no right of access to the classroom, nor do the police want such a right. However, any representation made by or on behalf of the local chief police officer (usually the Chief Constable or a nominee) must be considered properly by the governing body. Any failure in this respect could be questioned in the courts, as Mr Chris Patten, the then Minister of State for Education, pointed out in the Standing Committee during the passage of the Bill through Parliament.

## THE HEAD'S RESPONSIBILITY FOR THE CURRICULUM (s.18(3))

The Articles of Government provide that it is the Head's job to determine and organise the secular curriculum and ensure that it is followed. In so doing the Head will have to ensure that the curriculum of the school is compatible with the requirements of the National Curriculum, and take into consideration the LEA's and governors' policies. The Head must also have regard to any representations made by members of the community served by the school and the chief of police. The Head must also ensure that the curriculum is compatible with all other enactments relating to education, in particular those relating to children with special educational needs. Under the terms of his or her conditions of service, the Head is required to consult, where appropriate, the LEA, the governing body, the school staff and parents.

In view of the sensitivity of any issue involving the police, governors would be well advised to discuss the matter of school/police liaison with the Head and staff, as well as the parents. Appropriate training for teachers and police would be one important area of discussion.

The Association of Chief Police Officers and Society of Education Officers have published a report *Liaison between Police and Schools* following a joint working party on the subject. The National Union of Teachers has also published *Guidelines on Police/School Liaison*. Both of these documents set out the positive advantages to be gained from good relationships, although both make clear the sensitive nature of the matter.

Some further guidance is offered in the DES circular 7/87 Annex 10 *Relationships Between the School and the Police* which expresses the Secretary of State's hope that governing bodies and Heads will take advantage of the contribution which police officers can make to the classroom while confirming that the final decision on the detailed content of the curriculum rests with the school.

## THE CURRICULUM IN AIDED AND SPECIAL AGREEMENT SCHOOLS

These schools will also have to secure the implementation of the National Curriculum but here the onus is on the governors to "control the content of the secular curriculum" (s.19 of the 1986 Act), having had regard to the LEA's policy.

The governors will then allocate to the Head such functions as will enable him or her to determine and organise the curriculum and ensure that it is followed.

It is not clear what the difference is between the governors' "control" and the Head's "determination". What is likely to happen is that, as is usual now, the Head will present plans for the content of curriculum to the governors for their approval. The Head then settles and organises the curriculum on the basis of the content approved. Problems will only arise when there is conflict and there is little doubt that in such circumstances the governors' decision would prevail.

# WORK EXPERIENCE

All schools, including independent schools, must obtain LEA approval for work experience.

Heads should seek the agreement of the governing body as well as the permission of the LEA for work experience programmes.

The legal requirements are set out in the Education (Work Experience) Act 1973, which was followed by a helpful Circular 7/74 *Guidelines for the Work Experience Act 1973.*

# RELIGIOUS EDUCATION

## COLLECTIVE WORSHIP UNDER THE EDUCATION ACT 1944

All county and voluntary schools are obliged by s.25(1) of the 1944 Act to begin the school day with collective worship unless, in the opinion of the LEA (for county schools) or governors (if voluntary schools), the school premises make it impracticable. This could affect both large schools with small assembly halls and schools which have many religions or denominations. In county schools the collective worship must not be of any particular denomination, but in voluntary schools it must comply with the trust deed.

Parents have a right to withdraw their children from religious assemblies.

### Proposed New Arrangements for Collective Worship

The Government proposes to repeal s.25(1) of the 1944 Act in the Education Reform Bill 1987, where Chapter 5 retains the requirement for a daily act of collective worship but not necessarily at the beginning of the day. It is further proposed that there may be a single act of worship for all pupils or separate ones in different groups. It will be for the Head to make the arrangements after consulting the governors. Parents can request their children to be excused from such assemblies and until the request is withdrawn the pupil must be excused (s.25(4)).

## RELIGIOUS INSTRUCTION

Religious instruction must be given in every county and voluntary school (s.25(2) 1944 Act). However, the section does not say that religious instruction must be provided for all pupils, whereas the collective worship is specified as being "for all pupils". The implication might be that religious education should be provided for all pupils unless withdrawn by their parents. The Education Reform Bill 1987, in Chapter 1, reinforces the duty of LEA and governing body of maintained schools to ensure compliance with s.25(2) of the 1944 Act.

The religious instruction in county schools must be in accordance with the LEA's Agreed Syllabus which will have been agreed between the LEA, representatives from different denominations and teachers. Teachers are not obliged to teach religious education on conscience grounds and no teacher can be penalised for holding particular religious views. In controlled and special agreement schools there can be *reserved teachers* appointed by the governors for their fitness for teaching the particular religious instruction required. In controlled schools these cannot exceed one fifth of the staff and they can be dismissed if found incompetent in their instruction. In special agreement schools the number is settled in the original agreement. In aided schools all teachers should be appointed for their fitness to give religious instruction. In aided or special agreement schools the religious instruction must accord with the trust deed. If parents request the use of the Agreed Syllabus, arrangements can be made for their children either by the governors or LEA.

Teachers in aided schools and reserved teachers in controlled and special agreement schools appointed to give religious instruction can be dismissed if they fail to give the instruction efficiently and suitably (s.28).

## Parental Requirements

If a parent requires religious education different from that provided by the school the Act provides for the possibility of it being arranged in the school or elsewhere, where reasonably practicable (ss. 25-28 1944 Act).

# POLITICAL ISSUES IN THE CURRICULUM

The 1986 Act in s.44 provides that LEAs, governing bodies and Heads of county, voluntary or maintained special schools must forbid:

(a) the pursuit of partisan political activities by junior pupils (ie those of primary school age under 12)

(b) the promotion of partisan political views in the teaching of any subject in any school regardless of the age of pupils.

If the political activities for junior pupils take place off the school premises then a teacher arranging them (in the capacity as a teacher) or anyone else acting on the school's behalf must ensure that they are not partisan political activities.

## DUTIES OF LEA, GOVERNORS AND HEAD

It would not be sufficient simply to issue instructions forbidding these kinds of activities. It would be for governors, LEAs and Heads to ensure, as far as possible, that they did not take place.

However, a positive duty is laid on the same people, in s.45, to take reasonably practicable steps to ensure that where political issues are brought to the attention of pupils "they are offered a balanced presentation of opposing views".

Guidance on these topics is given in DES Circular 7/87 Annex 11 *The Treatment of Politically Controversial Issues in Schools*. Governing bodies, Heads and LEAs have to make judgements on what is a "balanced presentation" but it does not mean that a statement of all known viewpoints on every issue must be given. Pupils should be helped to understand why different people hold differing and opposing views and to analyse critically and evaluate their viewpoints. Books, posters, leaflets, etc used in the school should also show a reasonable balance.

In the Circular, the Secretary of State acknowledges the importance of the school's role in developing an appreciation of society's commitment to parliamentary democracy, freedom of the individual within the law, and the equality of all citizens under the laws. Governing bodies can include their views on political education in their statement of aims and could also modify any LEA policy on the subject. In so doing, governors would also have to bear in mind any representations by members of the community or chief of police, and any views expressed at the annual parents meeting. In aided and special agreement schools, the governors only have a duty "to have regard to" the LEA's policy (s.19 1986 Act).

# SEX EDUCATION

## SEX EDUCATION POLICY IN COUNTY, CONTROLLED AND MAINTAINED SPECIAL SCHOOLS

The LEA may or may not have a sex education policy, but governing bodies are not obliged to take any notice of it. It is for the governors to consider and determine the question of whether sex education should form part of the secular curriculum of the school, having consulted the Head. They must make a separate written statement of their sex education policy with regard to the content and organisation. If they decide that sex education should not form part of the secular curriculum they must make a written statement of that conclusion. The Secretary of State hopes that governors will be strongly influenced by the widely-held view that schools have a responsibility to their pupils to offer education on sexual matters. Governors should also take note that while the Head must ensure that the sex education in the school is compatible with the governors' policy, he or she does not have to do so where it is incompatible with syllabuses and requirements of external examinations (s.18(6)). Governors' policies will, of course, have regard to the age and background of the pupils.

LEAs, governors and Heads also have to take into account the provisions of s.46 of the 1986 Act which requires them "to take all reasonably practicable steps" to ensure that any sex education given to pupils is given in such a way as to encourage them to have "due regard to moral considerations and the value of family life". DES Circular 11/87, *Sex Education at School*, offers advice and guidance on sex education and governors would be well advised to refer to it when deciding their policy.

## SEX EDUCATION IN AIDED AND SPECIAL AGREEMENT SCHOOLS

The provisions of s.18 of the Education (No.2) Act 1986 that apply to other maintained schools (see above) do not apply to these schools. However, the Secretary of State hopes that governing bodies and Heads will bear in mind the guidance on Sex Education set out in Circular 11/87 *Sex Education at School*.

## AIDS

In the light of the general concern about AIDS, Circular 11/87 urges governors of secondary schools to pay particular attention to the part that education can play in combating it.

## HOMOSEXUALITY

During the committee stage of the Local Government Bill 1987, the government accepted a Conservative backbench amendment prohibiting the promotion in any maintained school of the "acceptability of homosexuality as a pretended family relationship". It was aimed at certain local authorities but all governing bodies, particularly in secondary schools, will have to consider the effect this might have on their sex education policy, and also the school's health education policy, since discussion about homosexuality is bound to figure in the fight against AIDS.

The DES have issued a factual booklet to schools entitled *AIDS: Some Questions and Answers*.

# THE CURRICULUM IN GRANT MAINTAINED SCHOOLS

## POWERS OF THE GOVERNING BODY

The powers of the governing body to determine the curriculum will be subject to two restraints:
  (a) the provisions in the Articles of Government made by the Secretary of State for securing the implementation of the National Curriculum in the School (Education Reform Bill 1987, Chapter 4)
  (b) any other provisions in the Articles concerning the curriculum (1987 Bill, Chapter 4).

However, since the grant maintained school is obliged to retain in the first instance the same character as it had prior to achieving this status general curriculum arrangements will already be in existence. In particular, it is likely that the same provisions of the 1986 Act about sex and political education will be applied to grant maintained schools as to LEA schools (see above).

### Complaints about the Curriculum in Grant Maintained Schools

The governing body will also be required in the Articles to set up a procedure to deal with complaints about any matter concerning the curriculum and in particular the implementation of the National Curriculum in the school (1987 Bill, Chapter 4).

# THE CURRICULUM IN CITY TECHNOLOGY COLLEGES

CTCs are, to all intents and purposes, independent schools. As in all independent schools governing bodies will be free to determine and implement the school curriculum as they think fit, but they will be under a statutory obligation to ensure that the curriculum is "broad with an emphasis on Science and Technology" (Education Reform Bill 1987, Chapter 5). In addition, they should also take note of the Secretary of State's urging of all independent schools to consider complying with the requirements of the National Curriculum.

The 1986 Act's provision with respect to sex and political education do not specifically apply to CTCs but governors should take note of the Act's provisions and the Circulars of Guidance that followed them (see above).

## PARENTS' RIGHTS WITH RESPECT TO THE CURRICULUM

Parents do not, in general, have the right to withdraw their children from parts of the school's compulsory curriculum unless the school agrees. However, they do have a specific right to withdraw their children from religious instruction and Assemblies of a religious nature by virtue of the provisions of the 1944 Act (see above).

Sex education is another area that has given rise to problems. There is no automatic right of withdrawal and often a discussion with the parent will allay fears.

The governing body can, however, in its sex education policy, give parents the possibility of opting out for religious reasons.

## CLASS SIZES

There are at present no statutory limits on class sizes although some LEAs have made local decisions on this. Normally, however, it is a matter for the Head to decide in the light of the school's ratio of staff to pupils. Nevertheless, governors in discharging their general oversight should be aware that safety, as well as educational considerations, must be a factor in determining how many pupils should be in a room with potentially dangerous equipment. Governors have a right to check what class arrangements the Head is making, even though it is the Head's responsibility actually to make the arrangements.

# Governors and Pupils with Special Needs

# 6

## CHILDREN WITH DISABILITIES

The education of children with disabilities is always a matter of particular concern to school governors, just as it is to many other groups. For 25 years after the Education Act 1944 was enacted the education of these children took place mainly in "special schools". However, over the years there has been growing unease about this practice as it appeared to concentrate on the handicap rather than the child's educational needs. In 1974 the Government set up a committee of enquiry chaired by the then Mrs Mary Warnock. Its report *Special Educational Needs. Report of Enquiry into the Education of Handicapped Children and Young People* (known popularly as the Warnock Report) was published in 1978. Amongst other things the report proposed that "special education" should become "a wider and more flexible concept" and that any child who needed help was one of special need. The integration of most pupils currently in special schools into ordinary schools was proposed, with such special schools having the role of educating pupils with severe or complex disabilities.

Governors have a duty to ensure that special needs are met within the school. They should know the main legal provisions and be aware of the school's need for training, resources and facilities in order to implement the new requirements.

## THE EDUCATION ACT 1981

Following the Warnock Report the 1981 Education Act made new far-reaching arrangements for children with special educational needs. As part of their direction of the conduct of the school, governors have a general duty to ensure that the requirements of the Act are met. Independent schools are excluded from the requirements and so far there is no indication whether the new grant maintained schools or City Technology Colleges will be included. Governors also have particular duties that flow from the Act and, therefore, need to know some of the main elements. DES Circular 8/81, *Education Act 1981*, explains the effect of the provisions of the Act. The main points are set out below.

### DEFINITIONS (s.1)

#### 1. Special Educational Needs

Children have special educational needs if they have learning difficulties which call for special educational provision to be made for them.

## 2. Learning Difficulty

Children have learning difficulties if:
- (a) They have significantly greater difficulties in learning than the majority of children of their age or
- (b) have disabilities which either prevent or hinder them from making use of educational facilities of a kind generally provided in schools within the LEA for children of their age or
- (c) are under five and could fall into either of the above categories if special provision is not made.

However, children are not to be taken as having learning difficulties solely because the language in which they will be taught is different from that spoken at home.

## 3. Special Education Provision

This is education that is additional to or different from the educational provision made generally by the LEA for children of that age.

Thus a child's needs have to be considered in the context of the needs and provisions made for other children.

## THE LEA'S DUTIES

The LEA has the duty:
- (a) to have regard for the need to ensure that special educational provision is made for pupils who need it
- (b) to ensure that children for whom *statements* are made (see below) are educated in ordinary schools provided that:
  - (i) account has been taken of the parents' views (including those of guardians and persons who have custody) and
  - (ii) education in an ordinary school is compatible with their receiving the special education they need, the provision of efficient education for the other children with whom they will be educated and the efficient use of resources.

## THE GOVERNING BODY'S DUTIES

The governors of county and voluntary schools must:
- (a) ensure as far as possible that any special provision required by a child is made
- (b) ensure that teachers in the school are made aware of the importance of identifying and providing for such pupils
- (c) ensure that where the *responsible person* (see below) has been made aware of a pupil's special educational needs, that those needs are made known to all those likely to teach that pupil
- (d) ensure that pupils with special educational needs have the opportunity to engage in activities along with children who do not have special needs, provided that this is reasonably practicable and that the conditions specified in (b)(ii) above are satisfied.

The *responsible person* would usually be the Head, but it could also be the Chairman of the Governors or another governor appointed by the governing body.

## IDENTIFICATION AND ASSESSMENT (ss.4 6 and schedule 1, part 1)

The LEA has the duty to identify those children with special needs and to issue guidance to schools on the procedures to be used in identifying and assessing the needs. Teachers, parents, doctors and educational psychologists will also be involved in the formal assessment.

The procedures are professional matters and do not involve governors directly. Governors should know that they are in existence and that the school has its own procedures.

## THE STATEMENTS (s.7 and schedule 1, part 2)

The detailed regulations made under s.7 are set out in the Education (Special Education Needs) Regulations 1983, (SI 1983 No.29).

After making an assessment an LEA must decide whether or not special provision should be made. If the LEA decides to do so then it must draft a proposed *statement of special educational needs*.

The statement must:
(a) describe the special needs
(b) describe the special provision required
(c) state the school which will meet the needs
(d) add details of any necessary additional provision.

Detailed guidance is given in the joint circular of the DES and DHSS *Assessments and Statements of Special Educational Needs* (DES Circular 1/83 31.1.83).

A High Court judgment held that speech therapy is not a special educational provision. It is possible that other disabilities might not be considered as requiring special *educational* provision.

## INVOLVEMENT OF PARENTS

Governors should be aware of the statutory requirements for parents to be involved at all stages, including the parents' rights to challenge the assessments, to appeal against the proposed provision to an appeals committee set up under the Education Act 1980 (schedule 2) and to request an assessment of their child on which LEAs have a duty to act unless they regard the request as "unreasonable" (s.9). It is also possible for parents to ask the Local Ombudsman (the Commissioner for Local Administration) to investigate the procedures of special needs appeal committees.

## SCHOOL ATTENDANCE ORDERS FOR CHILDREN WITH SPECIAL NEEDS

There are special arrangements for serving attendance orders on children with statements. In any dispute between an LEA and parents, the Secretary of State may give a direction and any direction to admit the pupil will be binding on the governors.

# THE NATIONAL CURRICULUM AND SPECIAL NEEDS

The Education Reform Bill 1987, in Chapter 1 provides that in respect of "statemented" children the National Curriculum requirements can be modified or disapplied altogether through the statementing procedure.

# SPECIAL SCHOOLS

## NEED FOR SPECIAL SCHOOLS

Although the trend in recent years has been away from segregation there is a continuing need for special schools and it is still true that the majority of statemented children are in special schools. Heads, staff and governors of such schools have considered their changing roles and in many cases new links have been forged with ordinary schools.

## CONDITIONS FOR APPROVAL

Special schools, whether maintained by a local authority or not, must comply with the Education (Approval of Special Schools) Regulations 1983, both in order to be approved as special schools and also while they remain in existence. In the main the regulations apply to special schools in hospitals except for one or two details concerning the premises and non-resident pupils.

The special educational provision must be approved by the Secretary of State, and where the school is not maintained by a local authority it must not be run for profit (r.2 and 3 of the 1983 Regulations).

Provision must be made for pupils' health, for pupils to attend religious worship, unless contrary to parents' wishes and for milk, meals and refreshment. Incident and punishment books must be kept and reports made to LEAs on pupils for whom they maintain statements.

There are further requirements relating to staff (r.13–16), to school accounts (r.17), making reports (r.18) and access by local authorities (r.19). A non-maintained special school is required to publish an annual prospectus (r.6 (3) and schedule 3).

The Secretary of State may withdraw approval if the school fails to comply with regulations.

## CONTINUING REQUIREMENTS

Further requirements for special schools are contained in the Education (Teachers) Regulations 1982 and the Education (Schools and Further Education) Regulations 1981 which aimed to achieve uniformity in the treatment of ordinary and special schools. The attention of governors of special schools is drawn to DES Circular 6/83, *The approval of special schools* (Welsh Office Circular 53/83) which contains detailed guidance on matters such as the composition of governing bodies; publication of information; admission; health of pupils; religious worship; milk, meals and refreshment; incident and punishment books; reports on pupils; staff; accounts; reports and returns; access to premises; approval of premises; duration of school year and day; leave of absence for pupils; transfer of records; withdrawal of approval; special schools in hospitals.

# CLOSURE OF SPECIAL SCHOOLS

In view of the changing scene a number of special schools have had to close and s.14 of the 1981 Act sets out in detail the procedure to be followed. (See Chapter 14.)

**REPORT OF THE EDUCATION, SCIENCE AND ARTS
COMMITTEE: MAY 1987**

This committee reported on the wording of the 1981 Act drawing attention to the need for extra resources for special education and the importance of "clear and coherent" LEA policies.

# STATEMENTED CHILDREN AT INDEPENDENT SCHOOLS

Under the 1981 Act, LEAs are now able to place pupils who are subject to statements in independent schools if they are approved by the Secretary of State as suitable for such pupils. These schools must meet standards similar to maintained and non-maintained special schools. HMI will visit the schools before approval is given. The details are set out in DES Circular letter *Placement of children with statements at Independent Schools* 16.6.83.

# Governors and School Discipline

# 7

## DUTIES OF THE HEAD AND STAFF

The duty to ensure good discipline in the school is the Head's aided by the staff of the school. S.22 of the Education (No. 2) Act 1986 sets out the duties of Heads of maintained schools in relation to the pupils:

(a) to promote self-discipline and proper regard for authority
(b) to encourage good behaviour
(c) to secure acceptable standards of behaviour
(d) to regulate conduct.

These are repeated in each Head's Conditions of Employment under the Education (School Teachers' Pay and Conditions) Order 1987 and, also by this Order, teachers are under an obligation to maintain good order and discipline among pupils and safeguard their health and safety, both when they are on school premises and when engaged on school activities elsewhere.

The governors may, if they wish, provide a written statement of principles of which the Head would have to take account.

The Head must also have regard to any guidance offered by the governing body. The standard of behaviour required could be determined by the governors, but in so far as it is not, then the Head determines it.

If any measures are likely to incur extra expense or affect the LEA's responsibilities as an employer, both the Head and governors must consult the LEA.

## LEAS' RESERVE POWERS

In a county, controlled or maintained special school, the LEA can take any necessary steps to prevent a breakdown of discipline caused either by the behaviour of pupils, or by any action taken by pupils at the school (s.28 of the 1986 Act).

If there is a similar threat in an aided or special agreement school, the governors and Head must consider any representation by the LEA (s.28(2)).

## PUNISHMENT IN SCHOOLS

Discipline in schools is inextricably bound up with the use of punishments. Until the 1986 Act most guidance about punishment came almost exclusively from case law.

## PRINCIPLES OF PUNISHMENT

The principles attaching to punishment in school were succinctly expounded by Mr Justice Phillimore in *Mansell v Griffin* (1908) 1 KB 947; LCT 216.

"It is enough for a teacher to be able to say — 'The punishment which I administered was moderate; it was not dictated by any bad motive; it was such as is usual in the school; and it was such as the parent of a child might expect that the child would receive if it did wrong'."

By virtue of the conditions of employment of school teachers and the fact that a teacher in the UK is considered to be *in loco parentis* and therefore assumes some of a parent's duties towards children in his or her charge, a teacher may take reasonable steps to ensure the discipline of the child, including reasonable punishment.

Governors usually become involved in such questions either in appeals against exclusion or in consideration of allegations by parents or students of unreasonable or excessive punishment from which may arise disciplinary proceedings.

## DETAILS IN SCHOOL PROSPECTUS

Governors should ensure that details of the disciplinary procedures, including the rules, punishments and sanctions used in the school, are contained in the school's prospectus. These are required by the Education (School Information) Regulations 1981.

# EXCLUSION OF PUPILS

There are substantial and detailed arrangements for school exclusion to which governing bodies are central. These are set out in ss.22 to 27 of the 1986 Act. The statutory requirements must be set out in the Articles of Government of maintained schools, as must any additional appeals procedures.

## TYPES OF EXCLUSION

There are now three types of exclusion on disciplinary grounds:
(a) *temporary* (or Fixed) — no more than five days in aggregate in any one term – more than five days in aggregate or where a pupil would lose an opportunity to take any public examination. A date would be fixed for a return to school.
(b) *indefinite* — no date fixed for return. This might be subject to conditions, eg signing a good behaviour contract.
(c) *permanent* — expulsion.

## THE HEAD'S DUTIES (ss. 22 and 23)

It is now made clear in s.22 that only the Head has the power to exclude pupils on disciplinary grounds. The Head must:
(a) decide which type of exclusion to make and, having made the order
(b) inform the parents (or pupil if aged 18 or over) of the nature of the exclusion, its length and reasons for it, and
(c) inform them of their right to make representations to the governing body or LEA.

In the case of a *temporary* exclusion, where it is longer than 5 days in aggregate in any one term or where a pupil may lose an opportunity to take an external examination, and an *indefinite* exclusion, the Head must *also* inform the governing body and the LEA giving reasons for the exclusion and its duration.

The Head can delegate this to a Deputy acting in the Head's name. The Head and senior management team must, therefore, consider the internal procedures needed. If the LEA directs reinstatement in the case of a temporary or indefinite exclusion the Head can make the exclusion *permanent*, thus bringing into play the formal procedures laid down in the Act (see below).

If the governors direct reinstatement then this is binding on the Head. If the Head receives conflicting directions for reinstatement from governors and LEA the direction that requires the earlier reinstatement must be complied with. The Head must also consider how best to guide the governors and LEA in ensuring fair play both for the school and the excluded pupil. This is a sensitive area requiring thought and discretion both by the senior management team and the governing body.

## THE GOVERNORS' DUTIES

The governors have a right to offer guidance to Heads on any disciplinary matters including exclusions. If they provide a written statement of general principles, the Head must act in accordance with it.

In particular the governors must review an exclusion once they have received notice of one from the Head. They will have to consider how they are going to fulfil their role. They may act as the whole body, or rely on the Chairman and/or Vice Chairman to take swift action on their behalf.

The Chairman (or Vice in the Chair's absence) has the option of seeking other governors' views on a particular exclusion (perhaps by canvassing members' views over the telephone as recommended in the DES Circular 7/87) or taking action personally as a matter of urgency and in all cases reporting back to the next meeting of the governing body for ratification. The governors have to decide whether to uphold the Head's decision to exclude or to direct reinstatement of the pupil. If they are satisfied with the exclusion they may simply note the position, but any procedure adopted must allow the governing body to act quickly either on their own account or in response to an approach by parents or LEA. The latter may wish to use its own power to reinstate a pupil.

In the case of *permanent* exclusions, if the LEA directs the Head to reinstate the pupil against the wishes of the governing body, then the latter may appeal to an independent Appeals Committee (see below). It is important for governing bodies to consider how far the procedures should be informal and conciliatory and at what point more formal measures are necessary. They might look to informal, conciliatory procedures in the early stages with more formal meetings later if necessary. In all cases the governors should remember that they are looking for a resolution to the problem, not simply a means of punishment.

## THE LEA'S DUTIES

The LEA's duties in respect of *temporary* and *indefinite* exclusions are as follows:

(a) *temporary exclusion* of not more than five days in aggregate in any term: the LEA would not not normally be involved in such an exclusion

(b) *temporary exclusions* of more than five days in aggregate in any term or where the pupil would lose the opportunity to take an external examination: here the LEA must decide whether simply to note the position or to direct reinstatement. If the LEA decides to direct reinstatement it must consult the governors beforehand. However, where a pupil has been excluded in circumstances which would prevent him or her taking a public examination and the LEA cannot contact either the Chairman or Vice Chairman of the governing body to consult him or her with a view to exercising their power to direct the Head to readmit the pupil, then the LEA may so direct the Head without consultation with the governing body (Education (School Government) Regulations 1987)

(c) *indefinite exclusions* here the LEA has the right to make directions if the governors do not intend to issue a direction, but must consult the governors before doing so. The LEA can direct reinstatement immediately, or within a specified period. If both the LEA and governors issue directions to the Head, the Head must comply with the direction that requires the earlier reinstatement *or* make the exclusion permanent which would bring in the procedures below.

## PERMANENT EXCLUSIONS

Here the procedures for voluntary aided and special agreement schools are different from those in county and voluntary controlled schools.

### County and Voluntary Controlled Schools

Only the Head can exclude permanently and must inform the LEA, governors and parents without delay. The governors must consider whether or not to direct reinstatement.

When the LEA has been informed of a *permanent exclusion* it must consult the governing body, consider whether the pupil should be reinstated immediately, reinstated by a particular date or not reinstated at all. If the LEA decides on reinstatement it must give a direction to the Head. Where it considers that he or she should not be reinstated it must inform the pupil (if at least 18) or parents.

### Voluntary Aided and Special Agreement Schools

Here the governors must consider reinstatement and direct the Head if they so decide. If they decide not to reinstate they must inform LEA and pupil (if at least 18) or parents. (s.25 1986 Act).

## APPEALS

In the case of county and voluntary controlled schools the LEA must make arrangements to enable a pupil (if at least 18) or parent to appeal against any decision not to reinstate following permanent exclusion and for the governing body to appeal against a direction to reinstate such a pupil. The governing body of an aided or special agreement school must facilitate its appeal by a pupil (if at least 18) or parent against its decision not to reinstate the pupil.

**Further Appeals**

Further appeals procedures for parents of excluded pupils in addition to the statutory ones concerning permanent exclusion, eg against indefinite exclusions, can be included in the Articles and any decision will be binding on the Head (s.27 1986 Act). If such a right is given by the Articles a person must be specified to whom an appeal should be made.

In addition to the appeals procedure provided for in the Articles of Government parents could also appeal to the Local Ombudsman (Commissioner for Local Administration) who is empowered to investigate the procedures of the Disciplinary Appeal Committees.

## DELETION FROM THE REGISTER

If a pupil is permanently excluded (and the LEA or, as appropriate, the governing body has decided not to reinstate) the pupil's name must be deleted from the school's register (Pupils Registration (Amendment) Regulations 1987).

# CORPORAL PUNISHMENT

## THE SCOPE OF THE ABOLITION

The abolition of corporal punishment was passed by the House of Commons on a free vote by a majority of one. This historic moment came in 1986 after centuries of ideological conflict about the sensitive issue and a gradual diminishing in the formal use of canes, tawses and other weapons. The abolition is contained in s.47 of the 1986 Education (No. 2) Act. It applies to:

(a) schools maintained by LEAs

(b) special schools not so maintained

(c) independent schools maintained or assisted by a government department such as Ministry of Defence schools and schools still receiving grants under the Direct Grant School Regulations 1959 (Education (Abolition of Corporal Punishment) (Independent Schools) Regulations 1987)

(d) places where the LEA provides primary or secondary education other than at school, eg home tuition, tutorial centres and withdrawal units and pupils on the assisted place scheme, music or ballet schemes or other local authority bursary schemes (by notice of the fees paid by the Secretary of State under s.100 of the Education Act 1944 or by the LEA under s.6 of the Education (Miscellaneous Provisions) Act 1953)

(e) any other category which may be prescribed by the Secretary of State.

Pupils whose fees are paid out of emoluments specifically provided for school fees (eg servicemen's children) are not included in the abolition.

The abolition also applies to Northern Ireland and Scotland.

**Independent Schools**

Apart from those mentioned above the abolition does not apply to independent schools and grant maintained schools, although most such schools are expected voluntarily to cease to apply it. Even so, independent schools cannot administer corporal punishment to state-funded pupils eg those on assisted places and cannot exclude, or refuse to admit, such pupils just because they are not liable to corporal punishment. They would run the risk of the Secretary of State terminating the participation agreement (s.47(a) of the 1986 Act). In addition, the European Parliament passed a resolution stating that schools must comply with the relevant provisions of the European Convention on Human Rights, which forbids, *inter alia*, the use of degrading punishment. In one case (*Campbell and Cosans v UK* 1976) the European Court held that parents have a right to forbid corporal punishment of their children.

## THE ABOLITION

S.47 achieves the abolition of corporal punishment by effectively removing the right of justification previously held by a teacher by virtue of being *in loco parentis*. As a result, corporal punishment is allied to battery.

As well as formal corporal punishment the abolition also includes non-formal uses of force as punishment, including slapping, throwing missiles and rough-handling.

# JUSTIFICATION FOR THE USE OF FORCE

S.47(3) of the 1986 Act recognises that sometimes teachers and others will have to use some physical force to prevent damage to person or property, eg when breaking up a fight. Teachers, after all, have a duty to maintain discipline and to safeguard their health and safety (School Teachers' Pay and Conditions Order 1987). Consequently, if the purpose of the physical force is to avert immediate danger to person or damage to property, a teacher will be protected if the action derives from mixed motives, since the Secretary of State does not wish teachers and others to hesitate in an emergency out of a fear that the action might be adjudged to include an element of punishment (DES circular 7/87). This is likely to cause more problems than the formal corporal punishments, since there will often be a fine line between punishment and justifiable restraint.

This is clearly a very sensitive area and will give rise to difficult exercises of judgement. If such matters come before governors they should take care to consider all the surrounding circumstances to ensure that the force used was reasonable.

# DETENTION

Detention is a time-honoured school punishment but the ultimate right to custody of a child rests with the parent (unless decided otherwise by a court). It amounts to false imprisonment for a child to be detained in opposition to a parent's wishes. However, teachers have the right reasonably to deprive children of their liberty by virtue of being *in loco parentis*, their express condition of employment to maintain discipline, and so long as detention is a normal punishment in the school, which is administered reasonably with due regard for the pupils' safety. Some LEAs have policies on its use and governors could include their own policy in their statement about discipline to the Head under s.22 of the 1986 Act. Heads and teachers would have to take account of the governors' and LEA's policies.

There are sometimes clashes between schools and parents over this issue, but the few cases that have reached the courts have tended to favour the school. Parents will be deemed to have accepted the school's sanction by virtue of having sent their children to the school and having read the prospectus containing details of the school's policy. Parents, however, are entitled to expect adequate notice that their child is to be detained and that there are good grounds for the detention to be inflicted, otherwise the punishment might not be reasonable.

## WHOLE-CLASS DETENTION

Teachers do not have a right to punish pupils indiscriminately and if a whole class is kept in because of the misdemeanours of one or two, it may well constitute unlawful detention of innocent people. Courts have been uncertain in their decisions on this.

In 1980 a Blackpool County Court judge held that it was reasonable to detain a class of 25 pupils for 10 minutes as a punishment for disruptive behaviour. He warned, however, that punishment must not be indiscriminate and such a "blanket detention" should only be used as a last resort.

# Governors and School Management

# 8

## RESPONSIBILITY FOR THE CONDUCT OF THE SCHOOL

The allocation of functions between the governing body, the LEA and the Head must be specified in the Articles of Government (s.16 of the Education (No.2) Act 1986).

The "conduct of the school" is under the direction of the governing body, subject to any provision of the Articles conferring specific functions on any person other than the governing body.

### SPECIFIC ALLOCATION OF FUNCTIONS

This is a very important provision. It means that the LEA cannot allocate to itself a blanket residuum of functions. All responsibilities that are not specifically allocated in the Articles will remain vested in the governing body.

### WHOLE ETHOS OF THE SCHOOL

The DES Circular 7/87 *Education (No.2) Act 1986: Further Guidance* points out that the governors must be concerned with the whole ethos of the school which includes many aspects, eg the school's general appearance; attitudes towards the school of pupils, parents and community; levels of parental support; quality of information put out and level of consultation on issues such as discipline. The Circular also draws attention to the Secretary of State's view that school uniform, if worn, contributes significantly to the ethos of a school and hence the question of whether or not it should be worn should be decided by the governing body. However, the use of disciplinary sanctions for pupils not complying with the school's requirements would be a matter for the Head to decide.

### HEAD'S RESPONSIBILITY

While governors have this general oversight of the conduct of the school, this should be distinguished from the Head's responsibility, set out in the Conditions of Employment of Headteachers (Education (School Teachers' Pay and Conditions of Employment) Order 1987) and repeated in the Model Articles for the "internal organisation, management and control of the school". This responsibility is subject to the provisions of the Education Acts 1944 to 1986, Articles of Government and, in the case of voluntary schools, any trust deeds. It is subject also to any rules, regulations or policies laid down by employers and any terms of the Head's appointment provided they are not inconsistent with the conditions of the 1987 Order. In carrying out his or her duties the Head must, *inter alia*, consult governing body (see Chapters 5 and 7).

# RELATIONSHIPS WITH THE COMMUNITY

The responsibility for the general conduct of the school enables the governing body to concern itself with the school's contribution to the community. In particular the Secretary of State hopes that governing bodies will consider the influence which the ethos and standards promoted by the school can have on the level of juvenile crime in the area, and will report on this in the annual report to parents. The Secretary of State believes that governing bodies should foster good relationships between the schools and local police (paragraph 5.9.3, Circular 7/87).

## RELATIONSHIPS BETWEEN THE SCHOOL AND THE POLICE

Annex 10 of Circular 7/87 draws together the various provisions in the 1986 Act concerning a school's relationship with the local police and offers further guidance.

The Secretary of State hopes that governing bodies will monitor the occurrence of vandalism in the immediate neighbourhood and will report this to parents in the annual report. The governors will also have to consider any representations made by the chief officer of police, in connection with that officer's responsibilities, about the secular curriculum of the school (paragraph 5.10.11 of the Circular).

The Head, too, must have regard to such representations (paragraph 4.10.19). The Secretary of State hopes that governors and Heads will take full advantage of the contribution that police officers can make in the classroom, although, of course, the final decision on the context of the curriculum and who should teach it rests with the Head (annex 10). (See also Chapter 5.)

The Association of Chief Police Officers and the Society of Education Officers have published a document *Liaison between the Police and Schools*, which has been circulated to all schools. Many LEAs and schools have now set up joint school/police liaison arrangements.

## DETAILS IN ANNUAL REPORT

In the annual report to parents (see Chapter 11) the governors must include details of steps taken to develop links with the community, including the police. Parents may question the governors' attitude towards the police and could also pass a formal resolution on the matter (ss.30 and 31 1986 Act and paragraphs 6 to 14 of DES Circular 8/86).

# SUPERVISION OF PUPILS

## DUTY OF CARE

Responsibility for children in a school's care goes beyond the legal and professional duty to teach them effectively. There is in addition the legal and moral duty to see that they come to no harm. This is the "duty of care" and since teachers are acting in the place of parents (*in loco parentis*) while pupils are in their charge, the standard by which the exercise of this duty is measured is that of a prudent parent in the context of the school. In order to achieve this high standard of care Heads have a legal responsibility through statute, common law and the school's Articles of Government to ensure that there is a safe and reliable system of supervision of pupils wherever they are engaged in authorised school activities, whether on the school premises or elsewhere, and that the system is effectively operated. Assistant teachers and any other assistants appointed for the purpose, have a legal duty to aid in this under the Head's direction.

## GOVERNORS' RESPONSIBILITIES

Governors have a duty under their general responsibility for the conduct of the school to ensure that there is an adequate system of supervision of pupils at all times and particularly at those times when there is large scale movement around the site, eg before school, during breaks and after school. It is the Head's duty to devise and implement the system. They also have a duty as employers in voluntary or independent schools to provide for the safety of anyone on the premises. (See Chapters 8 and 13.)

## BEFORE SCHOOL

Children tend to arrive at school anything up to half an hour before it opens and it would be unreasonable to expect the school to take responsibility for such unspecified lengths of time. It is usual to make clear in school prospectuses the time that the school will receive pupils and from that time the Head should lay down proper supervision rosters and procedures.

## MIDDAY SUPERVISION

This is dealt with below.

## AFTER SCHOOL

After school there should be similar procedures for supervising pupils leaving the site and those remaining on site for extra-curricular activities. A reasonable period might be 10 minutes but Heads have to make judgements about this and if the children are young and are usually picked up by parents it would be a legal duty to keep them securely on site until the parents arrive. Because the time a teacher spends looking after pupils is covered by the 1265 hours that can be directed by Heads, it is obvious that as well as formulating procedures, Heads must also make allowances for supervision time before and after school.

## THE SCOPE OF THE SCHOOL'S RESPONSIBILITY

The school's direct responsibility normally stops "at the school's gates", but not in all cases. For example, if a teacher saw a group of pupils either in danger or likely to cause danger to others, he or she would have a duty to exercise control. However, a teacher has no right or authority to stop traffic in order to allow children to cross the road. The local authority should provide crossing patrol wardens where there is a likelihood of danger.

## PREVENTING ACCIDENTS

Over the years there have been numerous accidents to pupils in classrooms, laboratories, gymnasia, sports fields and on school trips. Most of these have been pure accidents; some could have been prevented and others have been adjudged to be wholly or partly caused by negligence — of the owners of the school or employees. While it is the Head's responsibility to ensure that there are safe systems at all times that children are in the care of the school, the governors have a responsibility to watch over the carrying out of these and to intervene if they feel uneasy about them.

A useful rule of thumb might be to ask the question, "If I was a parent of one of the children, would I consider the school's system of control and procedures for ensuring safety to be reasonable and prudent, and likely to succeed?"

The answers are likely to take into account:

(a) the nature of the activity

(b) any hazards that could reasonably be anticipated

(c) the age and capabilities of the pupils

(d) the environment in which the activity would take place

(e) any safety factors that ought to be borne in mind

(f) any LEA procedures or codes of practice that the school should follow.

## REVIEW OF PROCEDURES

A high standard of care is expected from teachers and it is rare for teachers to neglect this duty. But, as with all systems, complacency can set in when the system has run successfully for some time.

Procedures for monitoring all systems should be built into each school's policy.

# HEALTH AND SAFETY

## GOVERNORS' RESPONSIBILITIES

The general responsibility of a governing body of a county, controlled or maintained special school stems from the Articles of Government. There is also a statutory duty under the Health and Safety at Work, etc Act 1974 for local authorities (or governing bodies of aided and independent schools) to make the premises reasonably safe for children as well as employees (s.3). A local authority could be held liable for any injury if it is found to have failed in its duty to provide safe premises. Consequently governors should issue written statements of safety policy or take note of the LEA's written policy and they must comply with any instructions provided by the LEA. They should also join with the Head and staff in monitoring the safety and security of the premises. It is usual for governors to require regular Health and Safety reports from the Head to help them to discharge this duty. Governors' recommendations should be passed on to the LEA unless it is the governors who are the employers and have responsibility for the premises. Guidance has been published by the Education Services Advisory Committee (ESAC) of the Health and Safety Commission: *Safety Policies in the Education Sector*, available from HMSO.

The Education (School Premises) Regulations 1981 lay down minimum specifications for maintained school premises which local authorities are obliged to uphold.

## THE GOVERNORS' POLICY STATEMENT ON HEALTH AND SAFETY

A policy statement might include the following:

(a) delegation of responsibilities to particular staff

(b) setting up a health and safety committee

(c) implementation of health and safety regulations
(d) implementing safety standards and safe working systems in various areas of the school
(e) availability and use of safety appliances and protective clothing
(f) responsibilities for monitoring compliance with the standards and procedures
(g) accident reporting and investigation
(h) employees' personal responsibility for health and safety
(i) duty of employees to co-operate with employer's policies
(j) ensuring the full briefing of staff on their responsibilities
(k) maintenance of appropriate records
(l) reports to the governors.

## STAFF TRAINING: HEALTH AND SAFETY

The Head must co-operate with the employers in ensuring that all staff have a basic training in:
– fire procedures
– other emergency procedures
– first aid and hygiene facilities
– understanding the possibility of hazards, eg in chemicals or machinery
– accident reporting procedure.

The general policies will come from the employers (LEAs or governors) but the implementation will be the Head's responsibility.

## SAFETY REPRESENTATIVES

Teacher and other employees' unions can appoint safety representatives in the school (Safety Representatives and Safety Committees Regulations 1977 SI 1977 No.500). If there are a number of unions represented in the school they must agree the number of representatives between them. The representative(s) should be reasonably experienced in the school. Small schools usually have only one representative but larger schools could have representatives for different areas or groups of employees, eg teachers and non-teachers.

### Duties of Safety Representatives

The representatives have a duty to investigate accidents and to take up any relevant issues with the Head and, if need be, the governors. They must be allowed time to carry out these functions and to receive training (Code of Practice, *Time off for the Training of Safety Representatives*). The Code of Practice *Safety Representatives and Safety Committees* recommends these representatives should keep themselves well informed of the employer's policies, legal requirements, likely hazards, and should carry out regular inspections.

A health and safety representative does not take on any extra legal liability by being a representative.

## SAFETY COMMITTEES

It is usual for large schools to have such committees but they are only obliged to do so if at least two safety representatives request one. The *Guidance Notes on Safety Committees* are useful in helping the committee to consider its task of ensuring health and safety at work.

The main functions are studying reports, assisting the development of safe systems, monitoring the systems and training employees. The committees can decide when to meet and how to conduct business. Minutes should be easily available.

## DRUGS AND SOLVENTS ABUSE

Secondary schools, by and large, have developed policies to combat drugs and solvent abuse both through health education programmes and by taking swift and appropriate action when instances occur. Governors are entitled to have a policy on the matter to which Heads would have to pay due regard. This whole subject is clearly one for professional and specialist input and one which governors should approach with sensitivity.

# SCHOOL MEALS AND MIDDAY SUPERVISION

## SCHOOL MEALS

S.22 of the Education Act 1980 allows LEAs to opt out of providing school meals in schools they maintain although they have the discretion to continue to provide meals and to charge for them. However, they must provide some kind of free meal for children whose parents are receiving family credit or income support. In addition they must provide facilities in the school for children to eat food brought from home.

## MIDDAY SUPERVISION

Teachers are no longer obliged to carry out supervisory duties during the midday break by virtue of paragraph 36 of the School Teachers' Pay and Conditions Document 1987 following on from DES Circular 5/85 *Midday Supervision* issued during the teachers' long pay dispute. However, Heads retain the legal responsibility for pupils on the school site during the midday break.

All supervision of the dining room and around the school is now subject to schemes involving persons, whether teachers or non-teachers, on separate contracts as midday supervisors. Even if they do not join the paid schemes, teachers can still volunteer to organise extra-curricular activities during midday breaks for which it is normal to receive a free lunch.

Governors are increasingly drawn into disputes about the inadequacy of many local authority schemes or the inability of LEAs to recruit sufficient numbers of suitably qualified supervisors. It is up to Heads, as the local agents on the spot, to use their professional judgement whether the premises are safe and secure and to make appropriate recommendations.

If a Head of such a school is worried about the safety of pupils on site all or some of them can be excluded until the position is adjudged to be safe. In doing so, however, the Head must be reasonably certain that their safety is not more at risk off the premises than on and must obtain LEA permission (or governors' permission in the case of aided or independent schools) to exclude them. Pupils who have a statutory right to a school meal could only be excluded after the meal had been provided. A Head who excluded pupils, even for good reasons, against the wishes of the LEA (or governors) might incur personal liability should there be an accident to a pupil.

The whole issue of midday supervision is a very thorny one. Heads and Deputy Heads in many schools have been compelled to cope with schemes which they consider inadequate. Even though governors may not have a specific duty to intervene, they do have a duty to help the school cope with midday supervision problems and to use their influence in persuading LEAs to implement schemes and to obtain sufficient competent staff to operate them.

## Governors' Control of Premises at Midday

Governors of county, controlled and maintained special schools are prevented from exerting control over the use of the school premises during the midday break (s.42 1986 Act). It is the LEA which must control the use of the school and ensure the safety of all those on site (see chapter 13).

# Governors and Finance

**9**

Governors of all schools have a general duty to watch over the finances of schools and to ensure that monies provided for the school are properly budgeted, spent and accounted for.

## CHARGING FOR SCHOOL SERVICES

Ever since the Education Act 1944 education in maintained schools has been understood to be free, since no fees may be charged (s.61 of 1944 Act). However, with the growth of activities that could not take place without parental contribution, eg residential field studies courses, individual music tuition, visits to theatres and concerts, the principle has become somewhat blurred. In view of this the Secretary of State will be including in the Education Reform Bill 1987 provisions which will enable schools to charge for certain educational services such as those mentioned above while yet preserving the essential free nature of the normal elements of school education.

## THE GOVERNING BODY'S DUTIES

The governing body of a maintained school has a duty to judge whether expenditure on the school represents economic, efficient and effective use of resources and has, therefore, a right to receive once a year from the LEA a statement of day-to-day running costs of the school and any capital expenditure either incurred or proposed (Articles of Government, following s.29 of the Education (No.2) Act 1986).

Governing bodies of all maintained schools are entitled to receive a sum of money from the LEA which they may spend at their discretion, although the LEA can impose reasonable conditions (s.29 (b)). For governing bodies of secondary and primary schools with more than 200 pupils the new Education Reform Bill 1987 contains more detailed duties and responsibilities (see below, Financial Delegation Schemes).

### ACCOUNTABILITY

The governors of maintained schools must include in their annual report to parents a financial statement summarising the latest financial statement provided by the LEA and indicate in general terms how the money provided by the LEA has been spent during the relevant year (s.30 1986 Act).

# FINANCIAL DELEGATION SCHEMES

Many LEAs have already initiated schemes of delegated financial control to schools and the Secretary of State has proposed, in Chapter 3 of the Education Reform Bill 1987, that all LEAs will have to prepare schemes setting out how they will allocate to each school a proportion of the annual aggregate expenditure on all schools in the authority. There must be a formula for allocation which can be determined by the LEA but one of the factors must be the number and ages of the pupils. In addition all LEAs must produce schemes to allow all secondary schools, and primary schools with over 200 pupils, the responsibility for managing their allocation. LEAs have the discretion to include smaller schools.

The governors will have to conform to any conditions or regulations laid down by the LEA for the management of the budget and auditing of accounts.

LEAs may suspend a governing body's right to take part, but the governors have a right of appeal to the Secretary of State.

LEAs will have to publish information about their schemes and make available special information to governing bodies.

The Secretary of State retains powers for specifying dates for schemes, for the determination and variation of the schemes, and the imposition of schemes.

Although the governors of schools involved in Financial Delegation Schemes will not incur any personal liability for anything done in good faith, they must ensure that the school has efficient systems for accounting for expenditure. The governors will be able to spend the school's budget share as they think fit (subject to any conditions laid down in the scheme) and may delegate all or part of their powers to the Head.

The limited financial delegation and information requirements of s.29 of the 1986 Act (see above) will have effect until the LEA schemes come into being and will continue to have effect for those schools not in the Financial Delegation Scheme.

# THE HEAD'S POWERS

Heads of all schools (whether in the Financial Delegation Scheme or not) may have all or part of the control of the finances delegated to them by the governors. In the case of Heads of schools not in the Financial Delegation Scheme this is contained in the Articles. Governors should, of course, require a proper account to be kept of the expenditure delegated to the Head.

The governors cannot incur any expenditure which in the Head's opinion would not be appropriate in relation to the curriculum of the school and, in the case of schools in the Financial Delegation Scheme, governors are expressly forbidden to incur expenditure which in the opinion of the Head would be inconsistent with the implementation of the National Curriculum (Chapter 3 of the Education Reform Bill 1987).

# RESPONSIBILITY FOR PRIVATE FUNDS

Schools usually have funds other than those provided by the state or local authority. There are such things as *trading accounts*, eg for the purchase of goods made by pupils or theatre tickets or foreign exchanges of pupils; *subscription funds*, into which parents pay a termly or annual amount; *charity funds, club and society funds* and so on.

As part of their responsibility for the general conduct of the school governors must ensure that all accounts kept by or in the school are properly run in accordance with LEA and their own regulations. It is common for the LEA and/or governors to require an audited annual statement of the income and expenditure.

In the governors' annual report to parents they must include details of the application of any gifts, including donations, to the school (s.30 of 1986 Act).


# INSURANCE

Employers or occupiers (whether LEAs or governing bodies or proprietors of independent schools) are responsible for ensuring that there is adequate insurance cover. The usual policies carried on a regular, annual basis are:

Premises
Public Liability
Employers' Liability
Personal Accident
and sometimes Damage to Personal Property.

There may be specific insurance cover required for particular activities, such as school trips and school minibuses. Where LEAs have a duty to maintain voluntary schools they will meet the necessary insurance costs.


# GOVERNORS' LIABILITIES

Governors will not be personally liable for the acts done by the governing body or any financial loss incurred by the school so long as they act in good faith. The governing body is, however, liable for any negligent act that they might perpetrate as employers. Consequently, adequate and relevant insurance policies should be in existence (see above).

## GOVERNORS' LIABILITIES IN GRANT MAINTAINED SCHOOLS

For schools which become grant maintained there are extensive provisions about the governors' responsibilities for grants and funds and their liabilities on the winding-up of the school (Education Reform Bill 1987).


# AUDIT

Maintained schools will normally receive visits by the LEA's internal auditors. They have the authority to enter the school, have access to relevant documents, require such explanations as are necessary and require any employee to produce cash or council property as necessary.

# GOVERNORS AS TRUSTEES

Some trust deeds of voluntary schools provide that all governors for the time being are trustees of the foundation. Because governing bodies now consist of a variety of different categories, the Education Act 1980 provided in s.5 that in such cases, only the governors appointed by the foundation and the governors appointed by the LEA or minor authority would be trustees of the funds of school foundations. For trust deeds coming into force after 1980 those drawing them up will be able to take into account the new composition of governing bodies.

# FINANCIAL RESPONSIBILITY: AIDED AND SPECIAL AGREEMENT SCHOOLS

The governing bodies are responsible for providing the equipment for these schools, the premises, the costs of any alterations required to bring the premises to the required standard and any repairs that are the governors' responsibility (s.15 1944 Act).

The Secretary of State is required to reimburse 85% of the expenditure on alterations and repairs and towards the provision of a site or buildings pursuant to proposals for a new or re-organised school under s.13 of the 1980 Act.

The LEA is responsible for the costs of staff even though they are not the employers.

# Governors and School Staff

# 10

## APPOINTMENTS, DISMISSALS AND DISCIPLINE OF STAFF

Each school must have a staff of teachers suitable and sufficient for the purposes of providing education appropriate to the ages, abilities and aptitudes of the pupils (Education (Teachers) Regulations 1982).

The governors' responsibility for the teaching and non-teaching staff begins with the selection and appointment of staff to the school. Procedures for county and voluntary schools, with effect from September 1988, are laid down in ss.34 to 39 of the Education (No.2) Act 1986 (repeated in Articles 14 to 20 of the Model Articles for county and maintained special schools, Articles 15 to 21 for controlled schools and 15 to 17 for aided schools). However, the Education Reform Bill 1987 contains further appointment, disciplinary and dismissal procedures for certain schools, overtaking those laid down in the 1986 Act. These schools are all county, controlled and special agreement secondary schools, and primary schools with over 200 pupils, which will automatically become part of the new statutory schemes for delegating financial management to schools. Local Authorities will have five years from the date of their financial delegation schemes to amend the schools' Articles of Government and thus, for the time being, the procedures below will apply to all schools as indicated. The proposed new procedures for the local financial management schools are set out at the end of the "appointment" section and the "dismissal" section of this book. For all other maintained schools the following procedures will continue to apply.

## EMPLOYMENT LEGISLATION

In addition to the specific employment laws relating to staff in schools contained in Education Acts, all employees in schools and their employers, whether LEAs or governing bodies, are subject to general employment legislation. The most important Act covering employment protection is the Employment Protection (Consolidation) Act 1978 as amended.

## QUALIFIED TEACHERS

Normally only qualified teachers can be employed in LEA schools but there are circumstances in which unqualified teachers can be appointed. These instances are contained in the Education (Teachers) Regulations 1982 which also set out the qualifications required of teachers of the deaf and blind.

**Section 11 Teachers**

Some teachers are known as "Section 11 Teachers". They are appointed to schools by local authorities who have been given grants by the Government to make special provision for the substantial number of immigrants whose languages or customs differ from the local community (s.11 Local Government Act 1966). Home Office Circular 97/82 sets out details of the administrative arrangements. All posts are subject to review by the Home Office.

# APPOINTMENTS IN COUNTY, CONTROLLED, SPECIAL AGREEMENT AND MAINTAINED SPECIAL SCHOOLS

## COMPLEMENT OF THE SCHOOL

It is up to the LEA to determine a complement of teaching and non-teaching staff for the school. Complement is a special term. It covers those posts for which the provisions of the 1986 Act and Articles govern appointments and dismissals.

The complement must include:
   (a) all full-time teaching posts at the school, and
   (b) all part-time teaching posts which are to be filled by persons whose only employment with the Authority will be at the school.

Thus all supply teachers and full or part-time teachers who are used by the LEA in at least one other school will not be on the complement of the school. As can be seen some posts are required to be on the complement; others are specifically excluded. The LEA can treat the remainder as it thinks best. The LEA can also review and change the complement from time to time.

Posts not on the complement are the responsibility of the LEA, subject to consultation requirements (s.35(2) of the 1986 Act). The complement of the school does not include any staff employed by the LEA solely in connection with either or both of the following:
   (a) the provision of meals
   (b) the supervision of pupils at midday.

Other non-teaching staff may be on the school's complement at the discretion of the LEA.

The point of the above regulations is to make clear which group of employees is to be appointed by the procedure laid down in the 1986 Act in which governors play a substantial role.

## CONTROL OF APPOINTMENTS

The LEA controls the appointment and dismissal of all teaching and non-teaching staff except for the special provisions for reserved teachers of religious education in controlled and special agreement schools which are covered by ss.27 and 28 of the Education Act 1944.

However, ss.37 to 39 of the 1986 Act specify the procedures for the appointment of Heads, the appointment of any other teaching or non-teaching staff on the school's complement and the appointment of Deputy Heads (see below).

If the LEA wishes to appoint other staff to work solely at the school, they must consult the governors and Head beforehand (except for those working only in the school meals service or as midday supervisors).

## APPOINTMENT OF HEADS

### Selection panels

The Articles of Government will specify the composition of the selection panel. However, there must be no fewer than three members appointed by the LEA and three by the governors. Whatever the number selected by the LEA, the members appointed by the governors must not be fewer than those of the LEA (s.36 and Model Article 17).

Under s.36(2) the Secretary of State has included in the Education (School Government) Regulations 1987 a regulation that the proceedings of selection panels for Heads and Deputies will be under the control of the panel and any questions decided by a majority with no members having a second vote. No Head can be appointed by an LEA unless recommended by a properly constituted selection panel (s.37).

### Method of appointment of Heads (s.37 of the Act and Model Article 18 for county schools)

1. If there is a vacancy for a Head the LEA has a duty to appoint an acting Head after consulting the governors.
2. It is the duty of the LEA to appoint a Head to a vacant post after consulting the governing body.
3. Before appointing a Head (other than an acting Head) the post must be advertised in publications circulating throughout England and Wales which the LEA considers appropriate.
4. The selection panel then selects the applicants to interview.
5. If there is a disagreement over which applicants to interview, the governors' representatives can select not more than two to be interviewed and the other members of the panel have a similar choice.
6. The panel can either recommend one of the applicants to the LEA or, if they cannot agree, try again, by repeating the selection and interviewing process as necessary.
7. If they still cannot agree, or decide that there is no point in repeating the process, they can require the LEA to re-advertise and, after re-advertising, repeat the selection and interviewing process.
8. If the LEA declines to appoint a person recommended by the panel, the panel must:
   (a) recommend another of the applicants interviewed by them, if they think fit
   (b) interview any applicants who have not been interviewed, whom they think fit
   (c) ask the LEA to re-advertise, if they think the post should be re-advertised, and then repeat the selection process.
9. The LEA must re-advertise where required to do so, and may do so if the panel fails to recommend a person acceptable to the LEA, or takes too long, in the LEA's opinion, over the selection.
10. The Chief Education Officer, or his representative, may attend all proceedings in order to give advice.

All of the above applies to the appointment of Heads, not acting Heads, who can be appointed as the LEA thinks fit.

## Appointment of a Head to a New School

In general the same appointment procedures will operate as under s.37 of the 1986 Act. However, paragraph 23 of Part III of schedule 2 of the 1986 Act gives LEAs a discretionary power where two or more schools are discontinued and a substantial number of pupils at these schools are expected to transfer to the new school. In this case one of the Heads of the discontinued schools may be appointed Head of the new school by the LEA after consultation with the temporary governing body, without going through the s.37 procedures.

## APPOINTMENT OF DEPUTY HEADS

The Articles must specify whether the selection procedure for Deputy Heads is to be the same as for Heads (see above) or as for assistant teachers (see below).

The guidance offered in Circular 7/87 *Education (No.2) Act 1986: Further Guidance* is that the choice of method should depend on the size and type of school. In view of the important managerial function of Deputy Heads in larger schools the procedures for appointing Heads would seem the most appropriate.

The Head, or acting Head, if not a member of the panel, is entitled to be present to give advice and, whether or not he or she attends, is entitled to be consulted by the panel before a recommendation is made to the LEA. There is no requirement in the Act for an Acting Deputy Head to be appointed pending the filling of the vacancy, but the LEA could include this facility in the Articles or simply allow schools to do so when the need arises.

## Appointment of a Deputy Head to a New School

If the procedure for Heads has been chosen for the appointment of a Deputy, then a Deputy Head may be re-deployed to a new school in the same way that a Head of a discontinued school could be redeployed under paragraph 23 of Part III of Schedule 2 of the 1986 Act (as above). If the procedure for appointing assistant teachers has been chosen, a Deputy Head could be redeployed to a new school from any school in the LEA as could any other teacher. The LEA has the discretion and the normal LEA procedures would be used subject to the specific requirements of the Act (see below).

## APPOINTMENT OF OTHER TEACHING AND NON-TEACHING STAFF

The appointment of any member of the teaching or non-teaching staff, other than the Head (or Deputy, if to be appointed by the Heads' procedure) must be set out in the Articles.

First of all the LEA must decide:
(a) whether to retain the post (if not a new one), then
(b) to advertise, or
(c) to redeploy existing staff.

### If the Post is Advertised

The LEA must make sure that persons qualified to fill the post (including their own employees) are given due notice.

The governors must choose applicants to interview, interview them and then recommend one of the applicants interviewed to the LEA for appointment. If the governors cannot agree they must repeat the process if they feel that is likely to lead to an agreement.

If they repeat the steps or have decided that it is not appropriate to repeat them, they must ask the LEA to re-advertise. They then repeat the process.

If the LEA declines to accept their recommendation the governors can recommend (or interview again and recommend) another applicant, if they think fit. Alternatively, they can ask the LEA to re-advertise and then repeat the process. The LEA must re-advertise if asked by the governors, unless the LEA decides to withdraw the post from the school's complement or decides to redeploy someone to the post. The Head and representative of the LEA are entitled to be present whenever governors meet to discuss or select applicants, for the purpose of giving advice.

### Redeployment

If the LEA decides not to advertise, the governors are entitled to draw up a job specification in consultation with the Head and send it to the LEA. The LEA must pay due regard to this and must consult the Head and governors when considering an appointment. If it makes an appointment with which the governing body disagrees the LEA must report this to the next meeting of their appropriate education committee.

## DELEGATION OF FUNCTIONS

The governors will have the power to delegate any of their functions above to:
  (a) one or more governors
  (b) the Head
  (c) one or more governors and the Head.

## TEMPORARY APPOINTMENTS

The procedure outlined above does not apply to temporary appointments which are awaiting the holder's return to work or made for the duration of the selection procedure. Other temporary posts would have to be filled as above.

## APPOINTMENTS IN NEW SCHOOLS

Appointments by temporary governing bodies will be via the same procedures as set out above.

## PROMOTION OF EXISTING TEACHERS

The procedures apply to appointments and not promotions of existing staff to the same post. The post may, of course, carry an Incentive Allowance or be a Main Grade post. The criteria for granting an Incentive Allowance are set out below. The procedures could be set out in Articles, given in the form of guidelines to governors, or left to governors.

# SELECTION PROCEDURES AND INTERVIEWS

Selection panels have a right to expect that applications are truthful and references honest. Application forms might ask for details of any criminal convictions received by the candidate. Even traffic offences should be listed. Applications for posts in schools are excluded from the provisions of the Rehabilitation of Offenders Act 1974 and therefore applicants are not entitled to withhold information about convictions, which for other purposes might be "spent". Governors should of course treat such information confidentially.

There are also procedures available to LEAs for police checks of possible criminal backgrounds of those who apply to work with children, in order to minimise future risks to children (DES Circular 4/86).

## FAIR INTERVIEW

Candidates have a right to a fair interview and in particular to encounter no bias on race or sex grounds. The selection panel's aim must be to select the appropriate candidate to fit the description of the post and ensure that each one is given fair and equal treatment.

## EQUAL OPPORTUNITY

All candidates, men and women, must have equal opportunities in obtaining a particular post. The Sex Discrimination Act 1975 recognises, however, that being a man or a woman can be a "genuine occupational qualification" (GOQ). The Act recognises the need for "decency" and it would probably be in order, for example, to offer a post of girls' PE teacher to a woman. The Race Relations Act 1976 is more restrictive but might permit the appointment of a teacher from a particular ethnic group to undertake personal counselling in a multi-ethnic school.

Each such case will have to be handled fairly and sensitively by the panel. In these as in other instances, the panel would be well advised to consider carefully the job specification and to take care in the requests for references and the questions put at the interview stage.

### Collection of ethnic statistics

Shortly there will be new regulations for the collection of ethnic statistics of teachers employed in schools. These are intended to help the government obtain a clear picture of the employment position and aid them in promoting a multi-ethnic teaching profession.

# DISMISSAL OF STAFF

## DISMISSAL OF STAFF WHO ARE PART OF THE COMPLEMENT (Model Article s.22 for county schools and 23 for controlled schools)

The LEA must consult the governing body and the Head (unless he or she is the person concerned) before dismissing an employee on the complement of the school, otherwise requiring them to cease work at the school or permitting retirement with entitlement to compensation for premature retirement. The LEA must also consider any such recommendations from the governing body.

## SUSPENSION OF A PERSON ON THE COMPLEMENT

Both the governing body and the Head have the power to suspend, without loss of pay, an employee on the complement when they consider such exclusion from the school to be necessary. If they do so they must inform the LEA and each other (as the case may be) and end the suspension if directed to do so by the LEA.

## EXTENSION OF PROBATION

The LEA must consult the governing body and Head before extending a teacher's initial period of probation or deciding whether it has been completed successfully.

# POSITION OF "RESERVED TEACHER" IN CONTROLLED AND SPECIAL AGREEMENT SCHOOLS

Foundation governors of controlled schools have additional rights in the appointment and dismissal of "reserved teachers" of religious education, ie teachers employed to give religious instruction other than in an agreed syllabus (s.27 1944 Act). If the LEA proposes to appoint a reserved teacher they must consult the governors. By virtue of s.28 of the 1944 Act foundation governors of special agreement schools have a veto on the appointment of reserved teachers. In the case of controlled schools, the governors must be satisfied as to the person's fitness and competence to give religious instruction before the appointment as reserved teacher can be made.

## DISMISSAL OF RESERVED TEACHERS

Foundation governors of controlled and special agreement schools have the right to require LEAs to dismiss reserved teachers if they have failed to give the efficient and suitable religious instruction for which they were appointed.

# APPOINTMENTS AND DISMISSALS IN VOLUNTARY AIDED SCHOOLS

## APPOINTMENT OF HEAD (MODEL ARTICLES, ARTICLE 15)

The governing body and not the LEA controls the procedure.
When there is a vacancy the governors must:
(a) advertise the post as they think fit
(b) draw up a short list
(c) interview those candidates short-listed
(d) appoint one of them where they think fit.
The LEA may prohibit the appointment if they are not satisfied with the educational qualifications of the candidate. If there is no suitable candidate the governors must repeat the process.
The Chief Education Officer or the CEO's nominated representative is entitled to attend any stage of the selection procedure to give advice.
Pending the appointment of a Head the governors must appoint an acting Head (Article 15(5)).

## Head's Contract

The governors must draw up a written contract of employment incorporating conditions of service. Apart from provisions relating to retirement or dismissal for misconduct or other urgent cause, the contract can only be determinable upon not less than:

(a) three months' prior notice in writing by either side taking effect on 30th April or 31st December; or

(b) four months' prior notice in writing by either side taking effect on 31st August.

## APPOINTMENT OF DEPUTY HEAD (MODEL ARTICLE 16)

The procedures will be the same as for Heads except that there is no obligation on the governors to appoint an acting Deputy Head in the event of a vacancy (Model Article 15(12)).

## DISMISSAL OF HEAD AND DEPUTY HEAD

The LEA may prohibit, in the Articles, the dismissal of the Head and Deputy Head without its consent. The only occasion on which this power can be overridden is if the Deputy has been appointed to give religious instruction other than in accordance with the "agreed syllabus" and has failed to do so efficiently and suitably. Here the governors may dismiss without the LEA's consent (s.28 1944 Act).

The Chairman or Vice-Chairman of the governing body has the power to suspend, without loss of pay, the Head or Deputy Head for misconduct or other urgent cause pending a decision by the governing body.

The governing body must dismiss the Head or Deputy if required to do so by the LEA. The Head or Deputy must be given at least seven days' notice of any governors' meeting called to consider the termination of his or her employment and is entitled to appear at the meeting accompanied by a friend. In any event note must be taken of the law on wrongful and unfair dismissal (see page 73–74).

## APPOINTMENT OF ASSISTANT TEACHERS AND NON-TEACHING STAFF (MODEL ARTICLE 16)

The LEA determines the number of assistant teachers to be employed and may give directions to the governors as to the educational qualifications required of assistant teachers employed to give secular instruction. With the agreement of the governors, the LEA may also include in the Articles a provision allowing the LEA to prohibit an appointment of a teacher of secular subjects (s.24 1944 Act).

Where there is a vacancy the governors can decide:

(a) to fill the post by the appointment of a person employed at another of the LEA's schools, or

(b) to advertise.

Governors are not obliged to appoint a person who has applied in response to the advertisement.

The governors determine the procedures to be used.

### Non-teaching Staff

The procedures for appointing non-teaching staff, with the exception noted below, are also covered by Model Article 16. The LEA may give directions to the governing body as to the number and conditions of service of such staff (s.22(4) of the 1944 Act). They will be appointed under a contract of service with the governing body and may be dismissed only by them.

School meals staff employed at the school are to be appointed by and may be dismissed only by the Authority.

## DISMISSAL OF TEACHING AND NON-TEACHING STAFF

The LEA may prohibit the dismissal of an assistant teacher without its consent except where the teacher has been appointed to give religious instruction other than in accordance with an "agreed syllabus" and has failed to do so suitably (s.28(2) of the 1944 Act). The governors retain the right to dismiss in this case. The procedures are the same as for Heads and Deputies (see above).

## TERMINATION OF THE CONTRACT BY TEACHERS

In normal circumstances assistant teachers may terminate their contracts only by giving at least:
  (a) two months' prior notice in writing by either side taking effect on 30th April or 31st December, or
  (b) three months' prior notice in writing by either side taking effect on 31st August.

# APPOINTMENTS AND DISMISSALS IN SCHOOLS IN THE FINANCIAL DELEGATION SCHEMES

## APPLICATION OF EMPLOYMENT LAW

The same employment law applies to schools in the Financial Delegation Schemes as to those not included. However, in Part IV of the Education Reform Bill 1987 it is proposed that the Secretary of State will have the power to modify such Employment Acts as he considers necessary.

## STAFF COMPLEMENT

The LEA will not be required to lay down a staff complement. Each governing body will decide within the resources available to it how many teaching and non-teaching staff to appoint.

## APPOINTMENTS IN AIDED SCHOOLS TAKING PART IN FINANCIAL DELEGATION SCHEMES

The governors have the power to appoint, suspend and dismiss staff as they think fit (1987 Bill, Chapter 3). Any other power or restraints that might arise from ss.22 and 24 of the 1944 Act will not apply.

The governors, or Secretary of State, may decide to involve the Chief Education Officer of the LEA, or a nominated officer, by sending an advisory report to that officer. If they do so the officer is entitled to attend all pre-selection and selection meetings concerning appointments.

Costs incurred by the LEA arising from the dismissal or premature retirement of a member of staff will not be met from the school's budget, unless the LEA has good reason for it.

## APPOINTMENTS IN COUNTY, CONTROLLED AND SPECIAL AGREEMENT SCHOOLS IN FINANCIAL DELEGATION SCHEMES

The appointment procedures are laid down in schedule 2 of the Bill.

### Appointment of Head and Deputy Head

1. The governors must notify the LEA of the vacancy and advertise the vacancy in publications circulating throughout England and Wales as they consider appropriate.
2. The governing body must then appoint a selection panel of at least three members, who will interview such candidates as they think fit and recommend to the governing body the appointment of one of the applicants where they consider it appropriate to do so.
3. The governing body, if it approves, must recommend the appointment to the LEA.
4. The LEA must appoint the person unless they are not satisfied that he or she meets staff qualification requirements applicable to this post. "Staff qualifications" mean:
   (a) qualifications
   (b) health and physical capacity
   (c) fitness on educational grounds or any other respect.
5. If the LEA declines to appoint the person, the governing body must recommend another person. The governing body can require the selection panel to repeat its process, with or without re-advertising, as they think fit.

The Chief Education Officer is entitled to attend any of the selection proceedings in an advisory capacity or to offer appropriate advice (schedule 2). The governors must consider the advice before making the selection.

### Appointment of Assistant Teachers

The procedure for appointing full-time or part-time staff is laid down in schedule 2 of the 1987 Bill, except where the appointment is a temporary one pending the return of the holder of the post, or held during the selection process.
1. The governing body determines a specification with the Head and sends a copy to the LEA.
2. The LEA may nominate for consideration a suitably qualified person in its employ or about to become employed by it.
3. The governing body may decide to appoint such a nominee, or to appoint someone in the school. If it does neither of these, it must advertise the vacancy in such a manner as to bring it to the notice of suitably qualified persons.
4. The governing body can delegate any of its functions to one or more governors, or the Head, or one or more governors and the Head acting together.

5. The governing body, or those acting on its behalf, must interview those candidates shortlisted and recommend an appointment to the LEA who may decline to make it if the person does not meet the staff qualifications (see above).
6. Where there is disagreement over an appointment the procedures can be repeated as appropriate.

The Chief Education Officer and the Head can attend any of the pre-selection or selection meetings in an advisory capacity. Before making an appointment the appointing panel must consider any advice given.

## Appointment of Non-teaching Staff

The governing body may recommend an appointment to the LEA. The LEA must appoint the person unless not satisfied that he or she meets the staff qualification requirements (see above).

## DISMISSAL OF STAFF IN SCHOOLS TAKING PART IN FINANCIAL DELEGATION SCHEMES

The Bill contains provisions for the governing bodies to determine that an employee should cease to work at the school. The governors must inform the LEA in writing of their decision and their reasons. If the employee is employed solely at the school, the LEA must then terminate his or her contract of employment. If the employee is not employed solely to work at the school the LEA must require him or her to cease to work at the school (schedule 2). The employee may also resign rather than wait for dismissal.

Any costs arising from the dismissal or resignation will have to be met by the LEA's retained budget and not from that delegated to the school, unless the LEA has good reason for deducting the costs from the school's budget (1987 Bill, Chapter 3).

## Suspension of Employees in Schools Involved in the Financial Delegation Schemes

Both the governing body and Head of such schools will have the power to suspend an employee without loss of emoluments. They must inform each other and also the LEA concerned when they exercise such a power. Only the governing body can end the suspension, which must be done in writing, and they must inform the Head and LEA immediately (schedule 2).

# WRONGFUL AND UNFAIR DISMISSAL

Employers, whether LEAs or Governors, must ensure that they have good reasons and use correct procedures before dismissing an employee in order that dismissals are not wrongful or unfair.

Wrongful dismissal occurs when the dismissal is in breach of contract, eg too little notice is given or contractual procedures are not followed.

Unfair dismissal may be claimed by certain employees who fulfil specified criteria. The most important ones are that employees must have at least two years' service and be below normal retiring age.

Dismissal for one of the following reasons can give rise to claims of unfair dismissal:

(a) because the employee joined an independent trade union

(b) because he or she has taken part in, or proposes to take part in, trade union activities at any appropriate time (ie outside working hours, or inside working hours by agreement with the employers)

(c) because of racial or sex discrimination

(d) on the grounds of pregnancy (NB an employer would have to find an employee a comparable post if her original post had gone during her leave of absence).

A dismissal might also be considered "unfair" if the procedures used were considered to be unreasonable. Governing bodies should ensure that the correct procedures are followed (see Articles) and that a fair hearing is given to the employee before dismissal is considered.

## REMEDIES FOR UNFAIR DISMISSAL

Unfair dismissal claims are made to an industrial tribunal. It is open to the industrial tribunal to dismiss the application or if it upholds it, to order reinstatement, or to order that the employee be re-engaged in a similar post, or to award compensation. The last is the most usual remedy.

## CONSTRUCTIVE DISMISSAL

Where an employer acts in fundamental breach of a term of an employee's contract, the employee may choose to leave and treat himself or herself as constructively dismissed. In such cases, claims are again made to an industrial tribunal and the remedies set out above apply to successful applicants.

# APPOINTMENT AND DISMISSAL OF THE CLERK TO THE GOVERNORS   (S.40 1986 ACT)

## COUNTY, CONTROLLED, SPECIAL AGREEMENT AND MAINTAINED SPECIAL AGREEMENT SCHOOLS

Standard provision for the appointment and dismissal of Clerks is made in Model Article 21 (22 for controlled schools).

The LEA must determine the arrangements for the appointment and dismissal of the Clerk after consultation with the governing body. Where previous Articles have allowed governors to appoint the Clerk, the Secretary of State would expect this provision to continue.

It is possible, but not mandatory, for the Clerk to be remunerated, in which case the remuneration could be borne by the LEA (Circular 7/87 paragraph 5.13.14).

The Clerk to a temporary governing body will continue as Clerk to the new governing body until a new appointment is made.

There may be special arrangements for controlled and special agreement schools.

## VOLUNTARY AIDED SCHOOLS

In such schools the governing body appoints the Clerk and may dismiss the Clerk. However, any remuneration for the duties in relation to the maintenance of the school will be determined by the LEA.

## THE POSITION OF CLERKS TO THE GOVERNING BODY IN SCHOOLS INVOLVED IN FINANCIAL DELEGATION SCHEMES (EXCEPT AIDED SCHOOLS)

When the Education Reform Bill 1987 becomes law, the appointment of the Clerks will be by the LEA, but the person will be selected by the governing body after consultation with the Chief Education Officer. The provisions also allow the governing bodies of all such schools to dismiss the Clerk. They must notify the LEA in writing giving reasons, and the LEA must comply on receipt of the governors' notification.

# APPOINTMENTS AND DISMISSALS IN INDEPENDENT SCHOOLS

Each school is free to operate its own appointments and dismissal procedures and to arrange its own conditions of service for staff. Many use the standard Governing Bodies' Association contract of employment. The normal employment protection legislation covers the employment of teaching and non-teaching staff in independent schools.

# CONTRACTS AND CONDITIONS OF SERVICE

## CONTRACTS OF EMPLOYMENT

Whether the employers are the LEA (county, controlled and special agreement schools) or the governors (aided and independent schools and, shortly, city technology colleges and grant maintained schools) the contract of employment for the teacher or non-teacher is regulated by the same basic law which governs all other contracts and the same employment protection legislation operates. All contracts have express (written) terms and implied terms; where there is a conflict between the two the written terms will take precedence.

There are fairly standard contracts for LEA schools, and most independent schools follow the model provided by the Governing Bodies' Association (for Heads) and AMMA (for teachers). The Catholic Education Council (CEC) has a standard form of contract for teachers in Catholic aided schools and the General Synod Board of Education has one for those in Church of England aided schools.

### Express Terms

The *Conditions of Service for school teachers in England and Wales* (the Burgundy Book) contains the majority of the agreed terms for local authority schools. This has now been supplemented by the *Teachers' Pay and Conditions Document 1987* (the Blue Book) which sets out a new pay structure and conditions of employment for teachers (see below). These conditions are also likely to apply to grant maintained schools and city technology colleges when the Education Reform Bill becomes law.

The terms and conditions of other non-teaching staff (the support staff) are governed by other national and local agreements. Governors need to be aware of the agreements in force covering their own school. There may also be local agreements between LEAs or governing bodies and employees.

It should be noted that Part IV "Miscellaneous Provisions" of the Education Reform Bill proposes that, for those schools involved in statutory financial delegation schemes, the Secretary of State may order modifications to any existing laws governing conditions of employment as he considers necessary and in particular those which confer powers or impose duties on employers, or confer rights on employees or otherwise regulate relations between employers and employees.

## Notification of Terms of the Contract

S.1 of the Employment Protection (Consolidation) Act 1978 provides that an employer must give an employee within 13 weeks of the employment beginning, a written statement containing, amongst other things, basic information about salary, intervals between payment, hours of work, holidays, pension schemes, sickness arrangements, the length of notice required before termination of the contract, and the title of the post. Any changes must be notified within one month.

## Implied Terms

In addition to the express terms every contract of employment automatically contains certain legal rights and duties which are implied into the contract. Every employee has a legal duty to obey his or her employer's directions, to give faithful service, to be honest, to protect the employer's interests and to keep any trade secrets that the employer might have.

The two main exceptions are:
(a) an employee cannot be ordered to break the law, and
(b) an employee may normally refuse to do work for which he or she has not been employed.

Otherwise, an employee risks dismissal for a breach of these implied conditions. The employee could also be sued for damages if the employee's breach of duty or negligence results in financial loss to the employer.

There are certain minimum rights for employees implied into contracts of employment. For employees in schools these are the rights: not to be discriminated against on grounds of race, sex or marital status; to receive equal pay as between men and women for like work or work of equal value. The employer also has the common law duties to pay full remuneration according to the contract, to take reasonable care of employees and to behave reasonably towards employees.

## Fixed Term Contracts

It is possible to appoint staff on fixed term contracts. In the case of teachers this is usually for one year at a time. Such teachers may have rights under the employment protection legislation, but many employers are now requiring them to waive their rights (in writing) to claim unfair dismissal or redundancy pay when being appointed. Such waivers are only effective if contained (in writing) in a contract for two years or more. Moreover, the waiver applies only if the employment ends because the fixed term has expired.

## Resignations

Employees may resign from their posts but must do so in accordance with any Regulations in force at the time (for teachers these are contained in the Burgundy Book) and any terms of their contracts (see above). Depending on the circumstances it is also possible for employers to offer employees the alternative of resigning rather than face dismissal.

## Notice of Dismissal

S.49 of the Employment Protection (Consolidation) Act 1978 sets out the statutory provision for periods of notice that employees must be given. In addition there might also be agreed periods in the employees' contracts.

## PROBATIONARY PERIOD

All qualified teachers in maintained schools must complete a probationary period as follows:
  (a) full-time teachers trained in the UK — one year
  (b) full-time teachers trained elsewhere — two years
  (c) part-time teachers — up to three years.

  The teacher has the obligation to prove ability but the employer has the responsibility for supervision. Nowadays there are senior staff in most schools, eg professional tutors, who have the responsibility for staff development and a varying range of training provision exists in all LEAs.

  Under s.41 of the 1986 Act a duty is laid on LEAs to consult governing bodies and Heads before either extending a period of probation or determining whether the probationer has successfully completed the probation (s.41(b)).

## MEDICAL FITNESS

A teacher or non-teacher at a school cannot be appointed to, or continue in employment at, a school unless the employer is satisfied as to his or her health and physical capacity (Education (Teachers) Regulations 1982).

  The responsibility for determining medical fitness of a teacher entering teaching rests with the employer. Circular 7/82 amending Circular 11/78 gives the details, the main points of which are contained in the Burgundy Book, Appendix III.

## PREMATURE RETIREMENT COMPENSATION

The agreement between LEAs and teacher organisations is set out in full in the Burgundy Book and incorporated in the statutory rights of employees.

# CONDITIONS OF EMPLOYMENT OF TEACHERS

The new conditions for teachers in England and Wales are contained in the *Blue Book School Teachers' Pay and Conditions Document 1987* which derive from the Education

(School Teachers' Pay and Conditions) Order 1987. Every school should have a copy, the contents of which are summarised below.

## DIRECTION OF THE HEAD

According to the Education (School Teachers' Pay and Conditions of Employment) Order 1987 teachers must carry out their professional duties under the reasonable direction of the Head (or the LEA if not assigned to a particular school) and such particular duties as may reasonably be assigned to them.

## PROFESSIONAL DUTIES

The following are the professional duties which a school teacher may be required to perform:

**Teaching Duties:**
   (a) planning and preparing courses and lessons
   (b) teaching pupils according to their educational needs, including the setting and marking of work
   (c) assessing, recording and reporting on the development, progress and attainment of pupils.

**Other Activities:**
   (a) promoting the general progress and well-being of pupils and classes
   (b) providing guidance and advice to pupils on educational and social matters and on future education and careers; making relevant records and reports
   (c) making records and reports on personal and social needs of pupils
   (d) communicating and consulting with parents of pupils
   (e) communicating and co-operating with persons or bodies outside the school
   (f) participating in meetings arranged for any of the above purposes.

**Assessment and Reports:** providing or contributing to oral and written assessments, reports and references relating to individual pupils and groups of pupils.

**Appraisal:** participating in any arrangements within an agreed national framework for the appraisal of a teacher's performance and that of other teachers. (The limitation of "an agreed national framework" means that teachers may not be directed to participate in other forms of appraisal. Teachers may, of course, volunteer to do so).

**Review; Further Training and Development:**
   (a) reviewing from time to time methods of teaching and programmes of work
   (b) participating in arrangements for further training and professional development.

**Educational Methods:** advising and co-operating on the preparation and development of courses, teaching materials, programmes, methods of teaching and assessment and pastoral arrangements.

**Discipline, Health and Safety:** maintaining good order and discipline, safeguarding pupils' health and safety both on the premises and when engaged on school activities elsewhere.

**Staff Meetings:** participating in meetings relating to the curriculum, administration or organisation, including pastoral arrangements.

**Cover:** supervising and so far as is practicable, teaching any pupils whose teacher is not available to teach them. However, no teacher shall be required to provide such cover:

(a) after the teacher has not been available for three or more consecutive working days
(b) where the fact that the teacher would not be available for a period exceeding three consecutive working days was known to the maintaining authority for two or more working days before the absence commenced; unless:
 (i) the teacher is employed wholly or mainly as a supply teacher, or
 (ii) it is not reasonably practicable for the maintaining authority to provide a supply teacher, or
 (iii) the teacher is a full-time teacher at the school but has been assigned by the Head to teach or carry out other specified duties (except cover) for less than 75% of the normal school hours in the week.

**Public Examinations:** participating in arrangements for preparing pupils for public examinations; assessing pupils for the purpose of such examinations and recording and reporting these assessments; participating in arrangements for pupils' presentation for and supervision during such examinations.

**Management:**
(a) contributing to the selection for appointment and professional development of other teachers and non-teaching staff
(b) co-ordinating or managing the work of other teachers
(c) taking part in the review, development and management of activites relating to the curriculum, organisation and pastoral functions of the school.

Most of the management tasks will be done by teachers who hold additional allowances but teachers on the basic scale may also be required to undertake management tasks.

**Administration:**
(a) participating in administrative and organisational tasks relating to the above duties
(b) attending assemblies, registering the attendance of pupils and supervising pupils before, during and after school sessions.

# WORKING TIME

## Number of Working Days

Teachers employed full-time in a maintained school (but *not* teachers employed wholly or mainly in residential establishments) now have to be available for work for 195 days in any year, of which 190 days are days on which the teacher may be required to teach pupils in addition to carrying out other duties. (The maximum number of sessions during which pupils have to be present at school is 380.)

The use of the other 5 "non-teaching" days is at the discretion of the Head, although the LEA may have a policy on the use of the days and may decide which days are to be designated "non-teaching days". The main use of these days is likely to be for in-service training.

## Maximum Hours

The maximum number of hours that a teacher may be required to work is 1265 hours, which must be allocated reasonably throughout the year including "non-teaching" days.

Time spent in travelling to and from the place of work does not count against the 1265 hours.

## Place of Work

A teacher must also be available to teach or perform other duties at such times and such places as may be specified by the Head (or the LEA if the teacher is not assigned to a particular school).

## Midday Break

Teachers cannot be required to supervise pupils during the midday break and must be allowed breaks of reasonable length either between sessions or between the hours of 1200 and 1400. They may, however, agree to be employed under separate contracts as midday supervisors for which they will be paid the LEA wages for such posts. They may also offer to run lunchtime activities but cannot be directed to do so.

## Additional Hours

In addition to all the other requirements set out above teachers are required under paragraph 36(1)(f) of the 1987 Order to work such additional hours as may be needed to enable them to discharge effectively their professional duties.

The paragraph gives examples such as marking pupils' work, writing reports and preparing lessons, teaching materials and programmes. There is no definition of the time to be spent on these. The time required will be that which is needed to complete the task. Although this seems to be open-ended, the amount of time needed will be determined by the teacher. This is a recognition of the professional nature of the work.

# TEACHERS' SALARIES

For some 75 years teachers' salaries have been settled in talks between employers and unions in The Burnham Committee. In 1987 all that changed. The Teachers' Pay and Conditions Act 1987 has given the Secretary of State powers to bring in a new system sometime in the future, with interim powers to make salary awards, advised by an Interim Advisory Committee nominated by himself. It is possible that in the future there will be different salaries in different regions (as there already are in London and the surrounding authorities where there is a system of "London allowances" on top of the general salary), and possibly higher pay for teachers of shortage subjects. The salary structure and pay scales existing at present have been laid down by the Secretary of State.

## Salary Structure

Under the Education (School Teachers' Pay and Conditions of Employment) Order 1987, the first order to be made under the Education Act 1987, all teachers, other than Heads and Deputies, are paid on an 11 point Basic Scale. On top of this, each school, according to the number of teachers on the complement, has a number of "Incentive Allowances", which can be added to particular teachers' basic salaries. These allowances range from A, the smallest to E, the largest. Teachers already receiving Scale 2, 3, 4 or Senior Teacher allowances on 30th September 1987 were automatically assimilated into the new scales. The new structure should be fully in place in 1990.

### Criteria for Allocation of Allowances

After October 1987 the new allowances will be given to teachers depending on the availability of an allowance in the school and the satisfaction of at least one of the following criteria:

(a) a responsibility beyond those common to the majority of teachers
(b) outstanding classroom teaching
(c) a shortage skill
(d) recruitment to a post difficult to fill.

As each school has a maximum number of allowances made available to it by the LEA within overall limits laid down in the Regulations, Heads, governors and LEAs will have considerable difficulty in dispensing these allowances judiciously.

# CONDITIONS OF EMPLOYMENT OF A DEPUTY HEADTEACHER
## PROFESSIONAL DUTIES

A person appointed deputy headteacher in a school, in addition to carrying out the professional duties of a school teacher, including those duties particularly assigned to him or her by the Head shall:

(a) assist the Head in managing the school or such part of it as may be determined by the Head
(b) undertake any professional duty of the Head which may be delegated to him or her by the Head
(c) undertake, in the absence of the Head and to the extent required by the employer, the professional duties of the Head
(d) be entitled to a break of reasonable length in the course of each school day.

# CONDITIONS OF EMPLOYMENT OF A HEAD
## OVERRIDING REQUIREMENTS

A Head shall carry out his or her professional duties in accordance with and subject to:

(a) the provisions of the Education Acts 1944 to 1986
(b) any orders and regulations having effect thereunder
(c) the articles of government of the school, *to the extent to which their content* is prescribed by statute
(d) where the school is a voluntary school, any trust deed applying in relation thereto and to the extent to which they *are not inconsistent with these conditions*
  (i)  provisions of the articles of government the content of which is not so prescribed
  (ii) any rules, regulations or policies laid down by his or her employers and

(iii) the terms of his or her appointment.

## GENERAL FUNCTIONS

Subject to the overriding requirements set out above, the Head shall be responsible for the internal organisation, management and control of the school.

### Consultation

In carrying out his or her duties the Head shall consult, where this is appropriate, with the authority, the governing body, the staff of the school and the parents of its pupils.

## PROFESSIONAL DUTIES

The professional duties of a Head shall include the following
**School aims:** formulating the overall aims and objectives of the school and policies for their implementation.
**Appointment of staff:** participating in the selection and appointment of the teaching and non-teaching staff of the school.
**Management of staff:**
  (a) deploying and managing all teaching and non-teaching staff of the school and allocating particular duties to them (including such duties of the Head as may properly be delegated to the deputy head teacher or other members of the staff) in a manner consistent with their conditions of employment, maintaining a reasonable balance for each teacher between work carried out in school and work carried out elsewhere
  (b) ensuring that the duty of providing cover for absent teachers is shared equitably among all teachers in the school (including the Head), taking account of their teaching and other duties.
**Liaison with staff unions and associations:** maintaining relationships with organisations representing teachers and other persons on the staff of the school.
**Curriculum:** determining, organising and implementing an appropriate curriculum for the school, having regard to the needs, experience, interests, aptitudes and stages of development of the pupils and the resources available to the school.
**Review:** keeping under review the work and organisation of the school.
**Standards of teaching and learning:** evaluating the standards of teaching and learning in the school, and ensuring that proper standards of professional performance are established and maintained.
**Appraisal, training and development of staff:**
  (a) supervising and participating in any arrangements within an agreed national framework for the appraisal of the performance of teachers who teach in the school (see above)
  (b) ensuring that all staff in the school have access to advice and training appropriate to their needs, in accordance with the policies of the maintaining authority for the development of staff.
  With respect to this duty it should be noted that teachers are not obliged to take part in any appraisal arrangements except within "an agreed national framework". The Secretary of State has reserve powers to make regulations requiring LEAs or anyone else he

prescribes, to appraise teachers' discharge of their teaching duties or any other activities connected with the school (s.49 of the 1986 Act).

The Regulations may prescribe that governors would have to

(a) ensure that the arrangements are complied with as far as is reasonably practicable

(b) provide such assistance to the LEA as it may reasonably require.

So far the Secretary of State has not issued any such regulations.

**Management information:** providing information about the work and performance of the staff employed at the school where this is relevant to their future employment.

**Pupil progress:** ensuring that the progress of the pupils of the school is monitored and recorded.

**Pastoral care:** determining and ensuring the implementation of a policy for the pastoral care of the pupils.

**Discipline:**

(a) determining, in accordance with any written statement of general principles provided by the governing body, measures to be taken with a view to promoting, among the pupils, self-discipline and proper regard for authority, encouraging good behaviour on the part of the pupils, ensuring that the standard of behaviour of the pupils is acceptable and otherwise regulating the conduct of the pupils; making such measures generally known within the school, and ensuring that they are implemented

(b) ensuring the maintenance of good order and discipline at all times during the school day (including the midday break) when pupils are present on the school premises and whenever the pupils are engaged in authorised school activities, whether on the school premises or elsewhere (see chapter 7).

**Relations with parents:** making arrangements for parents to be given regular information about the school curriculum, the progress of their children and other matters affecting the school, so as to promote common understanding of its aims.

**Relations with other bodies:** promoting effective relationships with persons and bodies outside the school.

**Relations with governing body:** advising and assisting the governing body of the school in the exercise of its functions, including (without prejudice to any rights he or she may have as a governor of the school) attending meetings of the governing body and making such reports to it in connection with the discharge of his or her functions as it may properly require either on a regular basis or from time to time.

**Relations with the authority:** providing for liaison and co-operation with the officers of the maintaining authority; making such reports to the authority in connection with the discharge of his or her functions as it may properly require, either on a regular basis or from time to time.

**Relations with other educational establishments:** maintaining liaison with other schools and further education establishments with which the school has a relationship.

**Resources:** allocating, controlling and accounting for those financial and material resources of the school which are under the control of the Head.

**Premises:** making arrangements, if so required by the governing body or the maintaining authority, for the security and effective supervision of the school buildings and their contents and of the school grounds; and ensuring (if so required) that any lack of maintenance is promptly reported to the maintaining authority or, if appropriate, the governing body (see chapter 13).

**Appraisal of Head:**
  (a) participating in any arrangements within an agreed national framework for the appraisal of his or her performance as Head
  (b) participating in the identification of areas in which he or she would benefit from further training and undergoing such training.

**Absence:** arranging for a deputy head teacher or other suitable person to assume responsibility for the discharge of his or her functions as Head at any time when he or she is absent from school.

**Teaching:** participating, to such extent as may be appropriate having regard to other duties, in the teaching of pupils at the school, including the provision of cover for absent teachers.

## DAILY BREAK

A Head shall be entitled to a break of reasonable length in the course of each school day, and shall arrange for a suitable person to assume responsibility for the discharge of functions as Head during that break.

## CONTROL OF STAFF CONDUCT

The conduct and discipline of school staff is of concern to Head, governing body and LEAs where applicable. All have a general duty to regulate staff behaviour, but in schools for which the LEA has the overall responsibility (county, controlled, maintained special schools) the LEA must exercise ultimate control and use of sanctions. However, in aided schools, grant maintained schools, city technology colleges and independent schools, the governing bodies have the duty to control staff conduct and the right to institute disciplinary proceedings.

In the 1987 Education Reform Bill the regulation of conduct and discipline of staff of schools involved in the new statutory Financial Delegation Schemes is given to the governing bodies. Each governing body will determine its own action in the exercise of this control or, if the proposed action is a function exercisable by the LEA and not themselves, the governing body can request particular action which the LEA is then under a duty to implement (Schedule 2).

### DISCIPLINARY PROCEDURES

Governors, either as employers or agents of the employer, must take great care that disciplinary procedures are carefully followed.

Teachers and any other employees can be disciplined or suspended or dismissed. Such misdemeanours as unexplained absence, poor time-keeping, insubordination, lack of preparation, refusal to obey a reasonable direction, unreliability, racial discrimination and misconduct can all lead to disciplinary proceedings or dismissal.

However, the law does provide safeguards through employment protection legislation. Acceptable reasons have to be given and proper procedures followed. Failure in any of these may lead to an appeal to an industrial tribunal or a judicial review by the High Court. The Ombudsman could also be brought into the matter.

## Suspension

Local authorities, or governing bodies where relevant, can suspend an employee from duty. This is usually where a criminal charge is pending or where children might be at risk. Suspensions are usually without loss of pay, but it is possible for suspensions without pay to be made, subject to the terms of the employee's contract.

## Disciplinary Codes of Practice

There is no national agreement in the teaching profession about appropriate disciplinary proceedings. However, all employees are entitled to know the rules which are applicable to them and so either LEAs or governing bodies must have known procedures. The Advisory, Conciliation and Arbitration Service (ACAS) has a useful Code of Practice giving advice on the preparation and operation of disciplinary procedures. It stresses that all employees should be told clearly what kind of conduct is expected of them and the consequences that might flow from breaking the rules. Essentially, the recommendations of the Code aim to ensure that the principles of natural justice are followed; that employees have a fair hearing, they have a full chance to defend themselves, are allowed to be accompanied by a colleague in any disciplinary hearings and have the right to appeal against any disciplinary sanctions imposed.

## Disciplinary Hearings

There is no nationally agreed format but since these hearings are quasi-judicial, employers, whether LEA or governing bodies, must have clearly laid down procedures that ensure a fair hearing before an unbiased panel. The only rules laid down in education legislation concern the withdrawal of certain persons during any such hearing. These are contained in the Education (School Government) Regulations 1987 (schedule II "Withdrawal from meetings"). (See Chapter 4)

## Misconduct of Teachers

High standards are expected of teachers and what might be acceptable in other walks of life could lead to disciplinary action in the teaching profession. Criminal convictions, sexual deviation, false claims as to qualifications have all at some time or other given rise to disciplinary action, including dismissal. At worst the Secretary of State can declare a teacher to be unfit to teach if there has been serious misconduct. The teacher's name is then placed on "List 99", which bars a teacher from teaching in both maintained and independent schools. For further guidance consult the DES Administration Memorandum 3/82 *Misconduct of Teachers*.

## Gross Misconduct

In cases of gross misconduct the normal disciplinary procedures relating to warnings can be by-passed and an employee can be summarily dismissed. It would still be necessary, though, to follow the principles of natural justice. It would be up to an employee to prove to an Industrial Tribunal that the dismissal was unfair.

## GRIEVANCE PROCEDURES

All employees are entitled to know how any grievance they have will be settled. The procedures agreed between teacher unions and local authorities are laid down in the *Conditions of Service of Schoolteachers in England and Wales* (the Burgundy Book). Variations for aided schools are included. Employers are free to build on this framework or make their own modifications.

It is very important that governing bodies should consider carefully the nature of their grievance procedures, and ensure that they are followed. In particular they should determine how any governing body meeting called to consider a grievance will proceed. Such a meeting is not a court of law and is primarily concerned with settling disputes and not apportioning blame. Nevertheless the parties in dispute need to feel that their views have been properly and fairly heard and considered. Full documentation of each side's view and evidence should be submitted to the panel and each other before any hearing.

There is no nationally agreed procedure for the actual hearing, but a possible format might be:

(a) Chairman's introduction and outline of procedure

(b) opening statement by the side with the grievance (this may be the employee or his or her friend)

(c) examination of the aggrieved person with questions designed to corroborate the salient points (witnesses could be called if appropriate)

(d) cross examination by the other side

(e) questions from the panel members (or these could be left to the end)

(f) opening statement by the side against whom the grievance is made

(g) examination of the client (if appropriate) — witnesses could be called and examined if appropriate

(h) cross examination by the other side

(i) questions by the panel members

(j) summing up by both sides with the aggrieved side having the right to the last word

(k) protagonists withdraw

(l) panel decides what to recommend.

Whatever procedure is used it should be made clear beforehand to the parties.

### Appeals

Both sides should know what arrangements there are, if any, for appeal.

## COLLECTIVE DISPUTES

In order to lessen the possibility of disputes between employers and employees, procedures for "collective disputes" have been developed. The possibility of conciliation should be available at local level through procedures agreed between employing authorities (whether LEAs or governing bodies or proprietors of independent schools) and representatives of the employees (usually union representatives).

Although the Council of Local Education Authorities and the teacher unions have stated a desire to set up a national conciliation body this has not materialised. The services of ACAS are available, however.

### The Governors' Role

Governors would need to take legal advice if they face such a dispute as employers. Normally it is LEAs which figure in a dispute with a teacher or non-teacher union, and the Head of the school who has to make appropriate adjustments to school routine primarily to protect the safety and welfare of pupils but also to minimise the disruption to their education. It is the governors' duty under their general responsibility for the conduct of the school to be as helpful as possible to the Head in meeting these requirements. They must at the same time recognise that great tensions will abound in these circumstances and careful and sensitive handling will be important. Therefore both LEAs and governors should take careful consideration of the view of the Head who is in the best position to appreciate the implications and ramifications.

# TRADE UNIONS AND PROFESSIONAL ASSOCIATIONS
## EMPLOYEES' RIGHT TO BELONG

All employees have a right to belong to a trade union, but the law only provides specific rights to trade unions and their members when they are recognised by an employer for negotiating purposes, which is the case in schools. These rights briefly are:
- to be consulted if redundancies are to be imposed
- for representatives to take time off work in connection with union duties
- to be given certain information
- to hold certain ballots on the employer's premises provided it is reasonably practicable.

The duty to provide information is covered in an ACAS Code of Practice entitled *Disclosure of Information to Trade Unions for Collective Bargaining Purposes*.

## TRADE DISPUTES

Trade Disputes (ie strikes or industrial action short of strikes) between employers and employees only attract immunity from civil actions for damages if they have been approved in a secret ballot and relate wholly or mainly to:
- conditions of employment
- engagement or suspension of employment
- allocation of duties
- discipline
- membership of a trade union
- facilities for trade unions
- consultation machinery.

## FACILITIES FOR UNION REPRESENTATIVES

Employing authorities and teachers' organisations have agreed on the facilities that representatives of teachers' organisations in a school should enjoy. Many of the rights are also contained in the Employment Protection (Consolidation) Act.

# Governors and Parents

## 11

## ACCOUNTABILITY OF GOVERNORS TO PARENTS

One of the main aims of the Education (No.2) Act 1986 was to promote an enhanced partnership between school, governors, LEA and parents; a process begun with the Education Act 1980. Many of the provisions will lead to greater participation by parents in school affairs, particularly through increased representation on the governing body and the introduction of statutory annual reports to parents and annual meetings for parents. Measures included in the Education Reform Bill 1987 for financial delegation and grant maintained schools will take the process even further.

## ANNUAL REPORT FOR PARENTS

The 1986 Act (s.30) requires Articles of Government to contain provisions for governing bodies to give each parent of registered pupils an annual report containing a summary of discharges of their functions during the year and any other such information as the Articles require. The report must be a straightforward factual document and must:

(a) be brief

(b) give date, time, place and agenda for the annual parents meeting (see below)

(c) include a note that at the meeting the governing body's, Head's and LEA's discharge of their functions will be discussed

(d) report on the consideration given to any resolutions passed at previous meetings

(e) name each governor and category, by whom appointed and date of end of term of office (except ex officio)

(f) give the names of Chairman and Clerk and where they may be contacted, eg school and education office

(g) announce arrangements for the next election of parent governors

(h) include a financial statement summarising LEA expenditure on the school and how the governors have spent their portion, plus details of any gifts (there are further requirements on financial information included in chapter 3 of the Education Reform Bill 1987)

(i) give details of public examinations as required by s.8(5) of the 1980 Act, ie those set out in the school's prospectus (see Chapter 12)

(j) describe steps taken to strengthen links with the community, including the police (see Chapter 8)
(k) draw attention to any information about syllabuses and other educational provision which might be required by regulations made by the Secretary of State.

## ANNUAL PARENTS' MEETING

Some two weeks after issuing the report the governors are obliged to hold a meeting to which all parents/guardians must be invited (s.31 of the 1986 Act repeated in Articles of Government). Governors of hospital or boarding schools may call such a meeting but it is recognised that it may be impracticable. Their justification for not convening a meeting could be covered in the annual report. The decision must be taken afresh each year.

The governing body decides who else should attend. In DES Circular 8/86, *Education (No.2) Act 1986*, it is suggested that governors should invite the Clerk, a few non-governor teachers and non-teachers, representatives of the LEA and, possibly in secondary schools, representatives of the pupils.

The purpose of the meeting is to discuss the annual report and the discharge of the functions of the LEA, the governing body and Head. Governors are urged, in the Circular, to create an atmosphere which enables parents and governors to engage in "full and businesslike discussions" from which no matter appertaining to the purpose of the meeting is excluded. It is recognised that an issue such as criticism of a named individual is particularly sensitive. Receiving such a point for further consideration by the governors or the LEA is suggested as an appropriate response. Any person criticized should be offered the right to reply either at the meeting or subsequently to the governors, the Head or to the LEA. If any criticism is regarded as defamatory it is probable that legal action would be successful only if it could be demonstrated that malice was intended (see Chapter 15.)

If the total number of parents present is more than 20% of the number of pupils at the school (ie if there are 200 parents present in a 1,000 pupil school) the meeting can pass resolutions which, if passed by a majority, must be considered by the governors at their next meeting. Governors may, at their discretion, allow resolutions to be taken even if there is less than 20% attendance.

# HOME-SCHOOL ASSOCIATIONS

Most schools now have some kind of Home-School Association, sometimes called Parent Teacher Association (PTA), but known also by other names.

Parents have no direct right to form such an association in the school's name nor to hold meetings on school premises. These are at the discretion of the governing body through its general responsibility for the conduct of the school and the accountability to parents. The governors also have a responsibility under s.42 of the 1986 Act to have a regard for the desirability of the premises being used by the local community.

If such an Association is formed, it would be well advised to have a formal constitution. This is essential if the Association is to register with the Charity Commission. A draft one is published by the National Confederation of Parent-Teachers Associations (NCPTA).

# OTHER CONTACT WITH PARENTS

Parents have a right to approach the governing body at other times in order to make proposals, recommendations, ask questions or register complaints. Minutes of meetings of governing bodies must be available to parents at the school as must the school prospectus (see Chapter 12) which includes the names of the governors and where the Chairman and Clerk may be contacted.

## INFORMATION ABOUT THE NATIONAL CURRICULUM

The Education Reform Bill 1987, in Chapter 1, provides that the Secretary of State may make regulations for even more information about the National Curriculum and other matters to be given to prescribed persons or persons in general.

# Governors and School Admissions

**12**

## ADMISSION PROCEDURES

Governing bodies tend to play a considerable role in admissions, particularly where schools are popular and oversubscribed. Great passions can be aroused in this field.

The law concerning admission is covered primarily in the Education Act 1980 supplemented by s.33 of the Education (No.2) Act 1986. These follow the general principle laid down in s.76 of the Education Act 1944 that as far as possible the Secretary of State and LEA must try to educate a child in accordance with the parents' wishes. These will be supplemented by new arrangements set out in the Education Reform Bill 1987 (see below).

LEAs and governors of aided and special agreement schools are required by s.38 of the 1980 Act to publish particulars of the arrangements for the admission of pupils to their schools. S.6 requires LEAs to enable parents to express a preference for a particular school and, subject to certain conditions, to comply with the preference. Parents may appeal against admission decisions to appeal committees that have to be set up by LEAs or governors in accordance with schedule 2 of the Education Act 1980.

## CONSULTATION REQUIREMENTS (s.33 1986 act)

Where the governing body is responsible for determining the admission arrangements they must consult the LEA at least once in every school year as to whether the arrangements are satisfactory, and also consult the LEA before altering them. It is up to the governors to initiate the consultation with the LEA. Where the LEA is responsible for determining arrangements for admission they must consult the governing body in the same manner.

The DES Circular 8/86 *Education (No.2) Act 1986* withdraws former advice that intake targets could be specified in approximate terms. The targets must now be specified precisely.

The circular also underlines the requirements for a clear statement of admission policies to be given to parents. Any criteria for admission should be clear and provide defensible bases for preferring one applicant to another.

## TRANSFER OF RECORDS (s.27 1980 act)

The governing body is required to transfer the records of a pupil who has left the school to the person responsible for the conduct of the new school, further education establishment or place of education or training if that person asks for such records (regulation 13 Education (Schools and Further Education) Regulations 1981).

Following regulations published in 1988 a maintained school or non-maintained special school must respond to a request by another school, whether in the public or private sector, to see a pupil's records (or a digest of them) when considering the admission of the pupil before the transfer.

# INFORMATION FOR PARENTS

The LEA, and governors of aided and special agreement schools, must publish information concerning the education available at the school (s.8 of the Education Act 1980). The information must be available at least six weeks prior to the final date for receipt of applications for admission or the date by which a preference must be expressed. The Education (School Information) Regulations 1981 list the information that must be included:

(a) the name, address and telephone number of the school and the names of the Head and Chairman of the governors

(b) the classification of the school as
   (i)   county or voluntary controlled etc
   (ii)  primary, middle etc
   (iii) comprehensive, grammar etc
   (iv)  co-education or single-sex
   (v)   day or boarding or both

(c) where appropriate, details of any special arrangements to be made for a child to visit the school before admission

(d) details of the school curriculum, including
   (i)   the curricula for different age groups
   (ii)  the subject choices, if any, and details of how such choices are made
   (iii) details of any sex education given (including the manner and content)
   (iv)  the level to which a particular subject is taught
   (v)   the careers education provided
   Note: (iv) and (v) are not necessary for primary, middle or special schools.

(e) the affiliations, if any, of the school to a religious denomination; the arrangements for religious education and details of how parents may exercise their right to remove their child from such education

(f) details of special curricular and other arrangements for particular classes, eg for pupils with special needs

(g) details of the organisation of education at the school, eg whether teaching groups include different ages and abilities together or in separate groups; arrangements concerning homework must also be included

(h) details of the pastoral care arrangements

(i) details of school discipline, in particular arrangements for bringing school rules to the attention of pupils and parents

(j) details of any clubs or societies and activities available outside the normal education provided

(k) the school policy on pupils' dress including, if appropriate, the arrangements for uniform and the approximate cost of each item of that uniform

(l) details of any advice or guidance concerning career opportunities, employment and vocations (not necessary in primary or middle schools)

(m) in Wales, details of the use of the Welsh language at the school, both by all pupils or by different age groups including

   (i) the use of Welsh for instruction in all or any subjects and whether alternative instruction in English is available

   (ii) the requirement for pupils to learn Welsh and arrangements for pupils excepted from this requirement

   (iii) the extent to which Welsh is used as the language of general communication within the school.

Attention should be drawn to any changes that are expected to occur after the start of the school year.

Schools which include pupils over 15 years of age (except special schools) must give the following information concerning public examinations:

(a) the school's policy concerning entering pupils for such examinations

(b) the public examinations for which pupils are most commonly entered

(c) the year at the school when most pupils take the public examinations

(d) the details of the last available year's results in GCE A and O level and CSE (in future, GCSE) summer examinations including the number of pupils in each year group that attained each grade (this should be subject by subject) and the total number of pupils in each year group (this figure should be the number on the third Thursday, or in Wales third Friday, in January, for each year group).

In the same regulations the LEA is required to publish information about the LEA's policy on such things as transport, transfer between schools, milk and meals, entry to public examinations and arrangements for special education needs.

# CATCHMENT AREAS

These are areas designated as attaching to particular schools and are an administrative method of regulating admissions. Parents, however, have a legal right to express a preference for a school outside the area in which they live (s.8 1980 Act). This includes schools in another local authority area.

# STANDARD NUMBERS AND THE EDUCATION REFORM BILL 1987 (PART I, CHAPTER 2)

The Education Reform Bill contains provisions for further constraining LEAs' and governors' ability to regulate admission numbers. This follows the Government's commitment to the enhancement of parental choice. When the Bill becomes law all county and voluntary schools will be required, at a specified date, to make arrangements to admit pupils right up to their available capacity. Governors and LEAs will not be able to decide to admit a number of pupils less than the school's *standard number*. The term *standard number*

is subject to detailed conditions and modifications in the Bill but what they add up to is that a school will be given a "standard admission number" for each age group which could be:
  (a) the number of pupils admitted in 1979
  (b) the number fixed when the school was formed (if later than 1979), or
  (c) if a higher number of pupils was admitted in the year preceding the coming into force of the new Act then that number would become the standard number.

Thus a school could possibly have more than one standard number, eg in a primary school one at 5 and one at 7 if it admits at that age from an infant school.

The LEA, or, as appropriate, the governors, can set a higher limit but not a lower one. Any dispute between governors and LEA can be remitted to the Secretary of State for resolution but before doing so the LEA and governors must consult each other about their differences.

Where either the LEA or governors consider that the school can no longer physically accommodate admissions of pupils at standard number level, they must first consult each other and whichever body is appropriate can then apply to the Secretary of State for a lower figure to be set. Such an application will be subject to a procedure involving the publication of the proposals and a two month objection period.

The appropriate admission authority (LEA or governing body) must keep the standard number under review and if the school's accommodation changes or the school's character changes in such a way as to alter the number of pupils for whom accommodation may be lawfully provided, then it will be possible for the standard number to be revised.

## THE SPECIAL POSITION OF PRIMARY SCHOOLS

Chapter 2 of the Bill removes the anomaly in the 1980 Act whereby a primary school's standard number might bear little relation to the actual number in the reception class in any one year because rising 5s are excluded from the calculations. The new legislation requires the standard number in a primary school to reflect accurately its physical capacity and therefore all children admitted into the reception class will count towards the standard number. Consequently parents of rising 5s can use the appeals procedure against admission decisions. But, by definition, children under 4 years 6 months are excluded since they are not rising 5s.

# REFUSAL TO GRANT A PREFERENCE

LEAs and governors are under a duty to comply with a parent's preference (s.6 (1) of the 1980 Act). However, a parental preference may be refused on grounds that:
  (a) compliance would conflict with arrangements made between the LEA and governors of aided or special agreement schools
  (b) admission is only by selection.

There is a further ground — "that compliance would prejudice the provision of efficient education or efficient use of resources" (s.6(3)(a)). This will not be available for schools whose admissions are below either the relevant standard number or any higher admission limit that has been fixed, once the provisions of the Education Reform Bill 1987 become law.

## RIGHT TO APPEAL

S.7 of the Education Act 1980 requires the LEA, or governors of aided schools, to make arrangements by which parents may appeal to an Admission Appeal Committee against a decision of the LEA or governors not to admit a pupil to the school of their preference. This Committee will be set up in accordance with schedule 2 of the 1980 Act. The appeals procedure is also set out there. The appeals must be held in private unless the governors or LEA responsible for the arrangements decide otherwise.

For aided and special agreement schools the Committee may include one or more governors.

It is now possible for parents to ask the Local Ombudsman (Commissioner for Local Administration) to investigate a complaint about the admissions procedure. It would also be possible for a parent to make a further appeal to the Secretary of State under s.68 of the 1944 Act if the parent considered that the appeal committee had acted unreasonably.

## REFUSAL OF ACCESS

Once a pupil has been admitted to a school he or she cannot be refused access except on reasonable grounds. These may be for such reasons as behaviour prejudical to discipline or on health and cleanliness grounds. In these and other cases it might be appropriate for other arrangements to be made such as home tuition or transfer to a specialist facility. Governors have a duty to ensure that the school has reasonable and appropriate arrangements for meeting these emergencies.

# REGULAR ATTENDANCE

Once admitted pupils are expected to attend regularly. The Pupils' Registration Regulations 1956 require the "proprietor", defined in s.114 of the 1944 Act as "the person or body of persons responsible for the management of the school", ie the governors, to keep an admission register and (except in independent schools where all pupils are boarders) an attendance register. In practice it is usual for LEAs to make the general arrangements and provide registers for schools for which they are responsible.

The details of how registers should be kept are in the regulations, but LEAs or governors could have their own policy concerning the actual marking of them since the regulations are silent on this. The deletion of the name of a pupil permanently excluded on disciplinary grounds is now covered by the Pupils' Registration (Amendment) Regulations 1987 (see Chapter 7).

The registers must be available for inspection by HMI, Officers of the LEA and anyone else specified by the Secretary of State.

## LEAVE OF ABSENCE FOR PUPILS: (EDUCATION (SCHOOLS AND FURTHER EDUCATION) REGULATIONS 1981)

Pupils cannot be granted leave of absence to enable them to take up employment, whether paid or unpaid, during school hours, except for "work experience" organised through the school, or where the child has obtained a licence to do so under the Children and Young Persons Act 1963.

Governing Bodies can, however, make arrangements to grant a request for leave of absence made by a parent to enable a pupil to go away on an annual holiday. This must not be for more than two weeks except in exceptional circumstances.

## LEAVING DATES

Pupils may leave school as follows:
1. Those reaching sixteen between 1st September and 31st January inclusive may leave on the last day of the Spring Term.
2. Those reaching sixteen after 31st January and by 31st August inclusive may leave on the Friday before the last Monday in May.

Pupils who have passed the date on which they could legally leave, can then leave (but not absent themselves without permission) at any time.

# ASSISTED PLACES

The Assisted Place Scheme is a means-tested scheme to assist those pupils who are considered academically able to benefit from an independent school education. It was set up by s.17 of the Education Act 1980.

The Education (Assisted Places) Regulations 1985 set out the criteria for assisted places at independent schools and revise the basis for remission of fees.

Only independent schools conducted for charitable purposes and providing secondary education are eligible to participate in the assisted place scheme. The total number of assisted pupils admitted to a school in any one year must include at least 60 per cent from publicly maintained schools, unless the Secretary of State has modified or dispensed with this requirement in any one year (s.19). Each school has to publish particulars of the scheme, the likely number of places, details of public examinations and results obtained in the same form as maintained schools under s.8(5) of the Education Act 1980 (see above) and any other information specified by the Secretary of State. LEAs are not able to veto pupils in their areas applying for or taking up assisted places.

A child can only be eligible for an assisted place if all the conditions in the regulations are satisfied, ie residential qualifications (s.4), age (s.5) income (s.7); conditions as to selection at Sixth Form level are in s.6. A school must also be satisfied that the child can benefit from the particular education provided by that school before selecting him or her, although the methods and procedures for selection are entirely a matter for the school to decide.

# REMISSION OF FEES

There are detailed regulations for the remission of fees in Part 3 of the regulations, and further regulations on financial matters in the *Education (Assisted Places) (Incidental Expenses) Regulations 1985*. The remission of fees refers to tuition fees and not boarding fees. The Secretary of State pays that part of the fees that the parents of the pupil do not.

# Governors and School Premises

# 13

## CONTROL OF SCHOOL PREMISES

During the school day, the responsibility for the use of the school premises is shared between the LEA, governors and Head, although the Head is likely to be directly in charge by virtue of his or her professional duties.

Outside school sessions and the midday break, the governors have control of the use of the premises, subject to any LEA directions (s.42 Education No.2 Act 1986).

At the midday break the LEA has control over the use of the premises with the Head acting as agent. This is an important distinction, as the supervision of pupils at midday is by persons employed on separate contracts, working under the direction of the Head.

Under s.22 of the Education Act 1980, governors must afford such facilities, premises and equipment as the LEA requires for the purpose of providing school meals.

During school sessions, the use of the premises is controlled by the Head whose job is to organise the curriculum of the school. He or she could therefore refuse the hiring of the school premises if it was likely to interfere with the curriculum arrangements.

The Head also has the responsibility, in his or her conditions of employment, for the security and effective supervision of the school buildings, their contents and school grounds, if so required by the governors or the maintaining authority.

## USE BY THE COMMUNITY

### COUNTY AND MAINTAINED SPECIAL SCHOOLS

Articles of Government must provide that the governors control the use of the school premises other than during school sessions or the break between sessions, subject to any direction given by the LEA. These directions cannot, however, be such as to remove the governors' responsibilities under s.42 of the Education (No.2) Act 1986. This section requires the governors to bear in mind the desirability of the premises being made available for use by the local community. Circular 7/87, *Education (No.2) Act 1986: Further Guidance* points out that community-use policies can enable much closer links to be formed between schools and the community.

The Sports Council might be of help when governors are considering community use of sport facilities. The Council might be willing to consider grant aid (Circular 7/87 paragraph 5.14.1).

LEAs could also apply for aid through the Government's Urban Aid Programme for dual use of facilities in inner cities.

The use of the premises by outside bodies is the responsibility of the LEA (or governors) and not the Head. Anything the Head does to facilitate use is on behalf of the LEA or governing body.

## AIDED AND SPECIAL AGREEMENT SCHOOLS

The LEA can require the governors to provide the premises free of charge for educational or youth purposes on weekdays when not in use by the school. These rights can be exercised on not more than three days per week. Otherwise the governors control the use of the premises but are responsible for any expenditure incurred when the activities are not connected with the work of the school. Letting fees for the school buildings will be kept by the governors but fees received for use of playing fields must be paid to the LEA.

## CONTROLLED SCHOOLS

Governors of controlled schools have a greater say in how the school is used at weekends. On Sundays the foundation governors can determine without restriction the use of the school (s.22 Education Act 1944).

## LETTING FEES

The governors of voluntary schools must pay to the LEA any letting fee received for the hiring out of any part of the school premises other than the school buildings (s.4(1) 1946 Act).

# USE OF SCHOOLS AT ELECTION TIMES

Under the Representation of the People Act 1983 the returning officer may use school premises for polling purposes. However, returning officers have been reminded by the Home Office that the law does not require the whole school to be closed.

Under s.95 of this Act any candidates at a parliamentary election may hold a public meeting as part of their election campaigns in a county or voluntary school, so long as it does not interfere with the educational use. A letting fee can be charged. However, under s.96 a similar meeting for a candidate at a local government election must be free of charge.

# LICENSING ARRANGEMENTS

Governors of all schools should be aware of the licensing arrangements to ensure adequate safety standards for public entertainment under the Local Government (Miscellaneous Provisions) Act 1982, and the Theatres Act 1968, which covers the public performance of plays, operas and musicals.

The Home Office view of what is "public" entertainment is contained in the statement *Public Entertainment Licensing and School Premises* May 1984. It would seem that according to the individual circumstances, an event organised by a school and attended by parents, teachers, school children and their families and guests would not be regarded as "public" entertainment. Governors might consider having a policy on this to help the Head in the decision whether to apply for a licence.

In the Greater London Area schools are covered in much the same way by the London Government Act 1963.

## LICENSING FOR THE SALE OF INTOXICATING LIQUOR

The Licensing (Occasional Permissions) Act 1983 provides that on not more than four occasions per year an occasional licence may be granted to an officer of an "eligible organisation" authorising him or her to sell intoxicating liquor at a function during a period not exceeding 24 hours. School fund-raising and Parents' Association activities would come under the head of "eligible organisations".

In addition the holder of a justices' on-licence may apply to a Magistrates' Court for an occasional licence to sell intoxicating liquor on premises other than his or her own.

# TRESPASSERS ON SCHOOL PREMISES

Trespassers are those who have no right to be on someone else's premises. Most people who come into school premises have tacit authority to do so but this authority can be withdrawn. Such people then become trespassers. Maintained schools can now deal with trespassers via s.40 of the Local Government (Miscellaneous Provisions) Act 1982 which makes it a criminal offence for a person to be on educational premises without lawful authority and cause a disturbance to the annoyance of those who lawfully use the premises.

# BUILDINGS AND MAINTENANCE

The School Premises Regulations 1981 give minimum criteria for buildings and recreational areas that must be met by September 1991. Governors should discover whether their schools meet the requirements.

If a building grant is sought, voluntary aided schools should send their applications via the LEA to the DES. In the case of church schools this will usually be done by the diocese. Sometimes, of course, voluntary bodies can meet the financial requirements without grant aid.

The DES is empowered to make loans to voluntary aided and special agreement school governing bodies at the same interest rate as Treasury loans to LEAs (s.105 of the 1944 Act).

Governors have a responsibility to monitor the state of the school premises and make reports to the LEA. It is particularly important that early notice should be given to LEAs where there is any defect likely to cause a safety hazard. In such circumstances it is normal for Heads to be able to take urgent action up to a limited sum of money.

## COUNTY SCHOOLS

The entire cost of maintaining the premises is borne by the LEA.

## AIDED AND SPECIAL AGREEMENT SCHOOLS

The governors must be able and willing to provide 15% of the cost of improving or enlarging the school to bring it up to the required standard or, if it is a new school, 15% of the school building.

The LEA pays for internal repairs. Governors are responsible for the external repairs to the school building with an 85% grant from the DES. The running costs of the school and the maintenance of playing fields, including any buildings on them, are the responsibility of the LEA.

## CONTROLLED SCHOOLS

In the case of these schools, governors are unable or unwilling to pay the 15% proportion of the cost of improving the school (s.15, 1944 Act). The maintenance costs are a charge to the LEA. Governors are responsible for expenditure incurred by them or by persons to whom they let the premises for activities unconnected with the work of the school, out of school hours.

# OCCUPIERS' LIABILITY

The LEA, or governors in the cases of voluntary and independent schools, have a responsibility for ensuring that the buildings and equipment are not defective. If an employee, a pupil or a visitor to the premises suffers any injury through any defective equipment, the LEA or governors may be liable for any damages arising from their negligence. The Occupiers' Liability Acts of 1957 and 1984 give an occupier "a common duty of care" to visitors. This extends even to trespassers if the occupier is aware that trespassers may be in some danger. The duty would be to take reasonable care that the trespasser did not suffer injury by, for example, posting notices or fencing off potentially dangerous areas.

# GRANT MAINTAINED SCHOOLS

The proposals for the new legal status of grant maintained schools (see Chapter 1) set out in the Education Reform Bill 1987 include the transfer of property, rights and liabilities of the former maintaining authority, whether LEA or governing body, to the new governing body (1987 Bill, Chapter 4). Grant regulations will follow and the maintenance and capital grants will be decided by the Secretary of State. However, the amount of any capital grant made will be equal to 100 per cent of the expenditure made. This contrasts with the 85% grant now paid to voluntary schools in similar circumstances.

Any proposals for a change in or enlargement of grant maintained school premises will require the Secretary of State's approval. He will also be empowered to authorise the transfer of such a school to a new site.

# Governors and the LEA

14

## GOVERNORS' AND LEA'S DUTIES

The LEA has a statutory duty to contribute to the spiritual, moral, mental and physical development of pupils by seeing that efficient education is available. The LEA must also ensure that there are sufficient schools available to fulfil this duty (Education Act 1944). It must also ensure regular attendance and make provision for school transport. There are other statutory duties laid on LEAs but, following the Government's stated aim to give more responsibility for schools to governing bodies, many powers have been transferred.

The sharing out of responsibilities between LEA and governors for a particular school will be set out in the school's Articles of Government (see Chapter 2), which is the main working document of governing bodies.

## DUTY TO COMPLY

The governing body has a duty to comply with the directions and policies that the LEA is legally empowered to make. Equally, an LEA cannot take upon itself a function that has not been specified in the Articles of Government (s.16 of the Education (No. 2) Act 1986).

## REPORTS BY GOVERNING BODY AND HEAD

S.32 of the 1986 Act provides that the Articles of Government should include a requirement for a governing body to furnish reports to the LEA in connection with the discharge of its duties.

The Head must also furnish to the governing body or LEA (as the case may be) such reports concerning the discharge of his or her functions as it may require. In the case of aided schools the LEA must notify the governors of any request for a report made to the Head. The Head must send a copy of any such report to the governing body.

## TRAVEL AND SUBSISTENCE ALLOWANCES FOR GOVERNORS

LEAs are empowered to pay travelling and subsistence allowances to governors. Members of a governing body in different categories of governorship cannot be treated differently, but the LEA could treat schools or other educational institutions differently, eg governors of a school could receive subsistence at a rate different from Further Education College governors (s.58 Education (No. 2) Act 1986).

## TRAINING FOR GOVERNORS (S.57 EDUCATION (NO. 2) ACT 1986)

All governors of maintained schools are entitled to a copy of the Instruments and Articles provided free of charge by the LEA and such other information as the LEA considers appropriate.

The LEA is also under a duty to make available (free of charge) such training as it considers necessary for the effective discharge of the functions of governors.

# REORGANISATION OF SCHOOLS

There are many reasons why individual schools, or schools in a particular area, might be reorganised, made larger, smaller or closed. The main consideration, however, is the number of pupils. The Audit Commission report, *Towards Better Management of Secondary Education*, pointed out that between 1979 and 1991 the number of secondary age pupils in England and Wales will fall by 27%.

## POLICY CONSIDERATIONS

The policy considerations for the reorganisation of maintained schools are set out in DES Circular 3/87 *Providing for Quality: The Pattern of Organisation to Age 19*. It identifies two issues which need to be addressed. The first is the effect of falling numbers of school pupils and the second is the need to make schools as cost-effective as possible. The effects of population change are further compounded by the increased weight given to parental preference for particular schools, as provided for in the Education Act 1980, and the open enrolment provisions which are included in Chapter 2 of the Education Reform Bill 1987.

## STATUTORY PROCEDURES

Statutory procedures must be followed when a school is opened, closed or altered significantly in size or character. The responsibility for the procedures rests with the LEA or voluntary body controlling the school.

## SIGNIFICANT CHANGE

It is for the Secretary of State to determine whether a change in the function or size of a school is so substantial as to be significant. Current guidance can be obtained from the Department of Education and Science.

## STANDARD NUMBER

When an LEA or voluntary body proposes to reduce the annual intake by more than 20 per cent of the *standard number* (see chapter 12), statutory procedures are necessary.

Where an LEA implements proposals to establish a new school, or to reduce the intake by more than 20 per cent, or to change significantly the character of the school, the standard number will be the one stated in the proposal.

No formal procedures are necessary:
  (a) if the standard number of a particular primary school is less than 20
  (b) in relation to the number of children younger than four years and six months.

## PROPOSALS

Under ss.12–16 of the Education Act 1980, s.14 of the Education Act 1944 and s.14 of the Education Act 1981 (in relation to special schools), proposals must be described in terms of establishing, ceasing to maintain, making a significant change of character in, making a significant enlargement to, or reducing the annual intake of, a school. However, the

Education Reform Bill 1987 proposes to repeal s.15 of the 1980 Act and will abolish the "significant reduction" category. The terms "reorganisation", "amalgamation" or "closure" do not appear in the legislation.

## County Schools

Under s.12 and, until the 1987 Bill becomes law, s.15 of the Education Act 1980, it is for the LEA to make the relevant proposals, which should include timings, details of numbers to be admitted and procedures for submitting objections. The proposals must explain the provisions available for displaced pupils.

## Voluntary Schools

Under s.13 and, for the present, s.15 of the Education Act 1980, it is for the voluntary body, or governing body, concerned to make proposals:
  (a) to establish a new voluntary school
  (b) to make any significant change in the character or significant enlargement of the premises
  (c) to reduce numbers in any age group to a number which is four fifths or less than four fifths of the "standard number" (see below).
The proposals must include the same details as for county schools.

The proposals to "cease to maintain" a voluntary school may be made by either the LEA under s.12 of the 1980 Act; or notice of discontinuance may be given by the voluntary body under s.14 of the 1944 Act. Proposals to "change the size or character" may be made only by the governors of that school.

## PUBLICATION OF PROPOSALS

Public notices must be published as soon as possible after the authority has adopted the proposals, in accordance with the Education (Publication of School Proposals) (No. 2) Regulations 1980. A copy of the proposals must be sent to the Secretary of State at this stage. The proposals will describe precisely how the LEA or voluntary body intends to carry out the changes.

## GUIDANCE ON PROCEDURES

General guidance on the procedures for "rationalising" schools under ss.12 to 16 of the 1980 Act is given in some detail in Annex 3 and its Appendices, of DES Circular 3/87.

## STATUTORY OBJECTIONS

Ten or more local government electors may object to the proposals as may any other LEA concerned. In particular, governors of voluntary schools should be aware that they can make statutory objections if their school is affected by proposals. Objections to proposals made by voluntary bodies must be sent direct to the Secretary of State.

If there are no objections the LEA must determine proposals for county schools within four months of their submission to the Secretary of State.

Further precise details about the determination and timings are contained in Circular 3/87.

## PROCEDURES FOR THE REORGANISATION OF SPECIAL SCHOOLS

Under s.14 of the 1981 Act an LEA's proposals to close a special school require the approval of the Secretary of State. In addition, an LEA must serve written notice of its proposals to cease to maintain a special school on:
  (a) the Secretary of State
  (b) the parent of every pupil at the school and
  (c) any other LEA which is served by the school for special education purposes.

The Secretary of State has the final decision ("determination") where a special school is concerned.

## POSITION OF TEACHERS AND NON-TEACHERS

Most LEAs now have a local reorganisation agreement worked out with the teacher associations which will allow for the redeployment of staff who lose their posts during reorganisation. There are sometimes similar arrangements for non-teachers. Statutory procedures are included in the Education (No. 2) Act 1986 in ss.35 to 39 (see Chapter 10).

## POSITION OF PUPILS

There will have to be special arrangements for pupils at the school affected by the reorganisation. Transport to and from school is often a particular concern. These matters should be clearly dealt with in the proposals and the governors should ensure that this is the case.

## POSITION OF GOVERNING BODIES

Where proposals to establish a new county school or to maintain a voluntary school have been determined, s.12 of the 1986 Act requires the LEA to institute a temporary governing body under an Instrument of Government. Schedule 2 of the 1986 Act makes detailed provisions for the governance of new schools (see Chapter 3).

# Special Issues

**15**

## EQUAL OPPORTUNITIES

Education Authorities have a reponsibility under the Education Act 1944, the Race Relations Act 1976 and Sex Discrimination Act 1975 to ensure that neither pupils nor employees, nor anyone else who comes into contact with the education service, encounter any discrimination on the grounds of race or sex.

Governing bodies have a duty to promote within their schools equality of opportunity both for teachers and pupils, and should have regard for any policy statement put out by the LEA.

## COLLECTION OF ETHNIC STATISTICS

The Secretary of State intends to issue regulations about the collection of statistics on the ethnic origins of teachers and pupils and has issued consultative papers on these. The intention is to learn more about the progress in schools of teachers and pupils with ethnic backgrounds that will be identified in the regulations, with a view to helping the DES to promote greater opportunities for ethnic minorities.

## SEX DISCRIMINATION

The following are aspects of the Sex Discrimination Act 1975 that governors should note.

It is unlawful for a "responsible body", ie LEA or governors, of an educational establishment to discriminate against a female pupil in making admission arrangements, providing facilities or by submitting her to any other detriment.

Governors must also ensure that they do not discriminate against any woman by treating her less favourably than a man. This includes pupils at school. Even single sex schools should provide the full range of subjects that should be available to both boys and girls, eg in a girls' school technology should be available. It is doubtful whether schools can lawfully deny a pupil access to particular sports solely on the grounds of sex. As far as school uniform is concerned, it would certainly appear to be against the spirit of the Sex Discrimination Act to prevent a girl from wearing trousers at school as some schools still do, although this has not been tested in the Courts.

There are exceptions in the Act for single sex institutions and where the essential character of the job makes it reasonable that the job should be done by a man or a woman, eg a PE teacher.

# SCHOOL TRANSPORT

Although most governing bodies are not themselves responsible for transporting pupils to and from school, nevertheless they are usually brought into disputes over school transport arrangements. The following particular issues seem to occupy governors' time.

## ENTITLEMENT TO SCHOOL TRANSPORT

The local authority is required to make arrangements to transport pupils who are not within "walking distance" of the school. There has been a good deal of case law concerning the definition of "walking distance" and the authority's obligation. S.39(5) of the 1944 Act defines the "walking distance" as two miles for children under eight years, and three miles for other pupils. Exactly where the measuring should start and finish has been a matter of judicial uncertainty. The most prevalent view is "the front door of the home to the front door of the school". However, any transport provided does not have to be "door to door" but reasonably near the home and school.

S.53 of the Education (No.2) Act 1986 amended the Education Act 1944 by requiring the LEA to consider the ages of pupils and the nature of the routes they could be expected to take in deciding whether or not they are required to make arrangements for transport. This requirement was considered in the case *Regina v Devon County Council* 1987. It held that the obligation to provide free transport for pupils of school age living outside "walking distance" from their school was absolute and that there would be a case for free transport if the routes were dangerous or, if the children should be accompanied, when it was not practicable to do so. A ruling by the House of Lords in 1986 stated that for a route to be "available" it must be one along which a child could walk to school, accompanied as necessary, with reasonable safety; but that it did not fail to be "available" because of dangers which would arise if the child was unaccompanied.

## THE NUMBER OF PASSENGERS ON A SCHOOL BUS

On any public service vehicle adapted to carry more than eight persons, seats may be considered "two thirds of a seat" in the case of children under 14. The Public Service Vehicles (Carrying Capacity) Regulations 1984 SI 1984/1406 provide that three children each under 14 years count as two passengers (regulation 5(2)(b)). A child is deemed to be under 14 until 31st August next following his fourteenth birthday.

## SCHOOL MINIBUSES

If a school decides to operate a minibus as a privately owned vehicle carrying passengers without any element of "fare contribution" then the school is freed from the details and rigours of public passenger vehicle licensing. The Minibus Act 1977, consolidated by S.19 of the Transport Act 1985, enabled schools and other bodies to run minibuses for the benefit of the community where the users were not members of the general public but might, none the less, contribute a "fare". The bus must not be operated with a view to profit, but operating charges can be recouped.

Under permit a school may operate either:
  (a) a small bus having 9 to 16 passenger seats for which a permit is available from the LEA, or
  (b) a large bus having more than 16 seats. Permits for these are only issued by the Traffic Commissioner.

The permit holder is responsible for ensuring that all the required undertakings are observed including roadworthiness, regularity of maintenance checks and fitness of drivers.

## THE SCHOOL YEAR AND THE SCHOOL DAY

Under s.21 of the 1986 Act school timings, terms and holidays for county, controlled and maintained special schools are determined by the LEA. The governors have a similar duty for aided and special agreement schools. Both are requested to consult each other before making a decision on such matters. (Circular 7/87 paragraph 5.11.2.). However, the Government is proposing to insert a clause into the Education Reform Bill making governing bodies of all maintained schools responsible for the timings of the school day.

The LEA has the power to require pupils to attend a place outside the school for the purposes of receiving any secular instruction and the governors of an aided or special agreement school have a similar power. These duties will be included in the Articles of Government.

Every day on which a school meets is divided into two sessions separated by a break in the middle, unless exceptional circumstances make this undesirable (r. 1 Education (Schools and Further Education) Regulations 1981). An expected amendment to the Education Reform Bill will permit variation by the governors in the arrangement of the school day. The minimum number of sessions is 380 in each academic year. The "academic year" is a period of twelve months from 1st September, unless the school term begins in August in which case it commences on 1st August. There is no provision for occasional holidays. (The Education (Schools and Further Education)(Amendment) Regulations 1987 SI 1987 No. 879.) Variations for schools meeting on 6 days are allowed for and nursery schools are not bound by the 1981 Regulations.

Through their Conditions of Employment, teachers have to be available for 195 days, 190 of these for teaching pupils and five for other activities directed by the Head.

Independent schools (including City Technology Colleges and possibly grant maintained schools) are free to determine their own timings, although in the case of CTCs and grant maintained schools they may be laid down in Articles of Government.

## DEFAMATION

There is a great deal of alleged defamation in the educational world. Instances abound of parents accusing Heads and teachers of libelling their sons and daughters in reports and references; Heads and teachers accusing the press, parents, local councillors and fellow teachers of making defamatory remarks. To no-one's surprise there are even cases of teachers accusing pupils of making defamatory remarks about them, and vice versa.

Governors are rarely directly involved in the accusations but they may often be the recipients of such a complaint and thus have the task of investigating it and acting as conciliators.

## THE DEFINITION OF DEFAMATION

Defamation is a complicated subject, but in a nutshell it requires a statement to be made which
  (a) tends to lower the person in the estimation of right thinking members of society generally
  (b) must be communicated to a third party
  (c) must be false.

## LIBEL AND SLANDER

Libel is defamation in a permanent form, eg written material, recordings. Slander, usually spoken, is defamation in an impermanent form.

Libel is actionable without any proof that damage has been caused, but slander, apart from a few specific cases, requires proof of damage.

## DEFENCES

The following are defences that are likely to be used in cases involving schools.

### Fair Comment on a Matter of Public Interest

Most aspects of education can be considered of public interest and so long as the person expressing an opinion believes the facts upon which the opinion is based to be true, he or she will have a defence.

### Justification

Truth of the statement is a complete defence. It will also suffice if it is substantially true.

### Unintentional

In such cases it is usual for the publisher of the alleged defamation to offer to make amends. If the offer is not accepted this could then be a defence.

### Qualified Privilege

This is the most likely defence in cases involving schools and might have application at the annual parents' meeting. It applies to most communications emanating from LEAs, governors and schools because the law gives protection to those who have a duty to make statements, or make reports of meetings. The defence can only be defeated if the plantiff can show that the statement was made to people who did not have a common interest in the subject matter, or that the defendant acted with malice, ie knowing that what he or she said was not true, or being reckless as to whether it was true or not.

## SETTLING CASES

It is usual in cases of alleged defamation to request a retraction and publication of an apology. It is possible to initiate legal action, but the cost is extremely heavy and the number of cases reaching the courts is small.

# GROUPING OF SCHOOLS

Under s.12 of the Education (No.2) Act 1986 LEAs may resolve that two or more schools shall be grouped together being treated as a single school with a single governing body.

The purpose of the provisions, according to the then Minister of State, Mr Chris Patten, speaking in Committee, was to allow the interests of two or more schools to be better served by a single governing body when they work closely together, eg a primary school and its "feeder" infant schools.

The group will be treated:

(a) as an aided school if it contains one or more aided schools
(b) as a special agreement school if it contains one or more such schools, and none of them is an aided school
(c) as a controlled school if it contains at least one controlled school and neither paragraph (a) nor (b) applies
(d) as a maintained special school if it consists only of such schools
(e) as a county school, if none of the above applies.

There are also provisions for review if there are changes in the status of any of the schools.

## REQUIREMENTS FOR CONSENT

Local education authorities have to obtain the consent of the Secretary of State to a proposed grouping of schools unless the group is to consist of only two primary schools in substantially the same area, neither of which is a special school and, in Wales, where there is no significant difference between them in the use of the Welsh language.

Where an LEA proposes to put a voluntary school into a group it must first obtain the *consent* of the governing body, and where a county or maintained special school is concerned the LEA must first *consult* the governing body.

The Secretary of State's consent may be given with such conditions as he sees fit.

## SETTLING OF DISPUTES

Disputes about whether two primary schools serve the same area or not, or whether there is a significant difference in the use of the Welsh language between two primary schools, will be determined by the Secretary of State.

Numerous details concerning the grouping of schools are contained in schedule 1 to the 1986 Act.

## PROCEDURE FOR MAKING THE INSTRUMENT OF GOVERNMENT (PARAGRAPH 2 OF THE SCHEDULE)

The LEA must consult each governing body in the group. If there is a voluntary school in the group the LEA has to secure the agreement of its governing body to the terms of the order and of the foundation governors to any provision of particular concern to them, and to have regard to the way those schools have been conducted.

## ELECTION OF PARENT AND TEACHER GOVERNORS (PARAGRAPH 3 OF THE SCHEDULE)

The Instrument of Government for any group may provide for the LEA to have the power to decide which parents and which teachers are entitled to stand in and vote at the election of parent and teacher governors. The LEA must ensure that all schools in the group will have had the opportunity to have participated in the election of at least one parent or (as the case may be) teacher governor of the group. This is a discretionary power for the LEA which it may include in the Instrument of Government for any group.

## GOVERNORS' ANNUAL REPORTS TO PARENTS (PARAGRAPH 4)

The governors of each school must prepare separate reports for each school in the group unless they decide to hold a joint annual parents' meeting. Any matters of particular interest to an individual school in the group must be treated separately in the report.

## JOINT ANNUAL PARENTS' MEETINGS (PARAGRAPH 5)

The governing body for the group may hold a joint parents' meeting for the grouped schools. If a joint meeting is held and separate annual reports have been made for each school, then all the separate reports must be sent to parents.

Where a proposal is put at a joint annual meeting which affects one or more, but not all, of the schools, only the parents of registered pupils at the relevant schools may vote on the question.

There still has to be a number of parents from an individual school equal to at least 20% of the number of pupils at the school, before a resolution to be passed that applies only to that school *must* be considered by the governors at their next meeting.

If there is any disagreement about which of the schools a proposed resolution concerns the Chairman of the governing body shall make the decision.

# CHANGE OF STATUS FROM CONTROLLED SCHOOL TO AIDED SCHOOL

S.4 of the Education (No.2) Act 1986 provides that governors of voluntary controlled schools can apply to the Secretary of State to become aided schools. The Secretary of State must be satisfied that the governing body is able and willing to meet the financial liabilities arising from aided status and to pay the LEA any compensation for capital expenditure (see below).

Foundation governors must consult the other governors and together they have to consult the LEA and publish their proposals. There is a two month period for objections to be made to the Secretary of State. The Secretary of State can then, by order, direct that from a specified date the school will be an aided school.

If the Secretary of State proposes to specify a starting date different from the one proposed by the governors, he must first consult the governors and LEA.

Further guidance on the procedures to be followed are contained in Annex 3 and Appendices in DES Circular 2/87.

## PUBLICATION OF PROPOSALS TO CHANGE STATUS FROM CONTROLLED TO AIDED

The *Education (Publication of Proposals to Change Status of a Controlled School) Regulations 1987* attached to DES Circular 2/87 provide that if a change is proposed under s.54(3) of the 1986 Act the publication of proposals must be:

(a) in at least one newspaper circulating in the school's area
(b) posted in at least one conspicuous place in the area
(c) posted on or near any main entrance to the school.

## COMPENSATION PAYABLE BY A GOVERNING BODY ON CHANGING FROM CONTROLLED TO AIDED STATUS

Where a controlled school becomes an aided school the governing body must pay the LEA such compensation for capital expenditure on the school as is agreed with the LEA or, failing agreement, as ordered by the Secretary of State.

Capital expenditure is defined as
- certain expense incurred by an LEA in establishing a controlled school (s.2 Education (Miscellaneous Provisions) Act 1953)
- expense incurred in enlarging a controlled school (s.1 Education Act 1946) or
- expenditure under paragraph 1 of Schedule 1 to the 1946 Act (Provision of buildings for voluntary schools).

Excluded from the requirement for compensation is any expenditure that could have been incurred if the school had always been an aided school.

Capital and external repair expenses incurred by governing bodies of aided schools attract an 85% contribution from the Secretary of State but no grants will be paid towards the compensation to the local authorities.

The Minister in Committee promised to look into the question of rights when latent damage is discovered after the transfer. It is likely that the principle of *caveat emptor* — "let the buyer beware" — will have to cover the question of rights if latent damage should be discovered after transfer.


# COPYRIGHT

The copyright regulations in this country are stringent and, in an age when reproducing written and spoken material is so easy, this causes problems for teachers, publishers and authors. The economics of teaching, being what they are, make it impossible to purchase original material all the time. On the other hand, the wholesale copying of copyright material is both morally and legally wrong. The law is currently governed by the Copyright Act 1956. It provides for literary, dramatic, musical or artistic work to be protected for 50 years after the death of the author and even particular editions or publications for 25 years. The Copyright (Computer Software) Amendment Act 1985 covers this new electronic resource.

A new Copyright Bill is expected to become law in Summer 1988. This will ease the problems of duplicating from books and recording off air.

## COPYRIGHT LICENSING AGENCY

Already in existence is a scheme for licensed copying of books, periodicals and journals through the Copyright Licensing Agency. Each maintained school should have a copy of the agreement and the instructions. The licence does not cover independent schools.

## GOVERNORS' DUTY

Governors have a duty to ensure that their employees do not break the copyright laws. The penalties, as some schools have discovered, are severe.

# RECORDS AND RECORD KEEPING

## PUPIL RECORDS

Regulation 13 of the Education (Schools and Further Education) Regulations 1981 requires a governing body to arrange for the transfer of pupils' school records when they have moved from one school to another or to a Further Education Establishment (see Chapter 12). During 1988 the Secretary of State intends to make Regulations concerning the keeping and disclosure of pupil records, under powers granted by s.27 of the Education Act 1980, the primary aim of which is to allow parents access to records kept on their children.

Schools will be required to keep records of pupils' educational progress year by year but it is unlikely that the detailed content and format will be specified.

The regulations do not affect independent schools.

These proposals refer to manual records. Records kept on computers are subject to the access provision of the Data Protection Act 1984 (see below.)

## DISCLOSURE OF RECORDS

Schools will be obliged to allow parents of pupils under 18 (but not the pupils themselves) access to the information held. Pupils over 18 will be entitled to have access, except for access to a statement of special educational needs which they have no right to see (Education Act 1981).

Personal records kept by a teacher are not expected to be included in the Regulations, except where these records are passed to another teacher, in which case they will in all probability be liable to be made available to parents.

It is likely that governors will have the responsibility for making arrangements for the keeping and disclosing of such records but that day-to-day responsibility will rest with the Head.

## PROTECTION OF INFORMATION ON DATA-PROCESSING MACHINES

The Data Protection Act 1984 controls the use of all personal information processed by electronic data-processing equipment.

Information about staff and pupils is increasingly being stored on school computers and from November 1987 everyone has had the right (for a fee) to obtain a copy of most of his or her personal data held in such a manner. Records of special education needs are governed by different rules (see Chapter 6).

The Act requires all users of electronic data-processing equipment to ensure that all personal data stored in the machines is under adequate security and that statutory rights to its access are facilitated.

All school computers used for storing any kind of personal details must be "registered". Maintained schools will normally be registered by the LEA and must, therefore, follow its guidelines. Governors of independent schools must also ensure that the provisions of the Act and the regulations are complied with.

A number of guides have been published by the Data Protection Registrar, obtainable from the Registrar's office (see list of addresses).

# Main Statutes

## ACTS OF PARLIAMENT

1. Education Act 1902
2. Education Act 1944
3. National Health Act 1946
4. Copyright Act 1956
5. Occupiers' Liability Act 1957
6. London Government Act 1963
7. Local Government Act 1966
8. Theatres Act 1968
9. Education (Work Experience) Act 1973
10. Rehabilitation of Offenders Act 1974
11. Health and Safety at Work etc. Act 1974
12. Sex Discrimination Act 1975
13. Race Relations Act 1976
14. Minibus Act 1977
15. Employment Protection (Consolidation) Act 1978
16. Education Act 1980
17. Education Act 1981
18. Local Government (Miscellaneous Provisions) Act 1982
19. Representation of the People Act 1983
20. Licensing (Occasional Premises) Act 1983
21. Occupiers' Liability Act 1984
22. Data Protection Act 1984
23. Transport Act 1985
24. Copyright (Computer Software) Amendment Act 1985
25. Education (No.2) Act 1986

### TEXT REFERENCE

The 1902 Act
The 1944 Act

The 1980 Act
The 1981 Act

The 1986 Act

## GOVERNMENT BILLS

1. Copyright Bill 1987
2. Education Reform Bill 1987
3. Local Government Bill 1987

'GERBIL' or Bill 1987

## MAIN STATUTORY INSTRUMENTS

1. Pupils' Registration Regulations 1956 (SI 1956 No. 357)
2. Independent Schools' Tribunal Rules 1958 (SI 1958 No. 519)
3. Direct Grant School Regulations 1959 (SI 1959 No. 1832)
4. Safety Representatives and Safety Committee Regulations 1977 (SI 1977 No. 500)
5. Local Government (Voluntary Schools and Educational Charities) Order 1973 (SI 1973 No. 2025)

6. Education (Publication of School Proposals) (No.2) Regulations 1980 (SI 1980 No. 658)
7. Education (Middle Schools) Regulations 1980 (SI 1980 No. 918)
8. Education (School Information) Regulations 1981 (SI 1981 No. 630)
9. Education (School Premises) Regulations 1981 (SI 1981 No. 909)
10. Education (Schools and Further Education) Regulations 1981 (SI 1981 No. 1086)
11. Education (Teachers) Regulations 1982 (SI 1982 No. 106)
12. Education (Particulars of Independent Schools) Regulations 1982 (SI 1982 No. 1730)
13. Education (Special Educational Needs) Regulations 1983 (SI 1983 No. 29)
14. Education (Approval of Special Schools) Regulations 1983 (SI 1983 No. 1499)
15. Public Service Vehicles (Carrying Capacity) Regulations 1984 (SI 1984 No. 1406)
16. Education (Assisted Places) Regulations 1985 (SI 1985 No. 685)
17. Education (Assisted Places) (Incidental Expenses) Regulations 1985 (SI 1985 No. 834)
18. Education (Publication of Proposals to Change the Status of a Controlled School) Regulations 1987 (SI 1987 No. 34) (attached to Circular 2/87 27 March 1987)
19. Education (Grants) (City Technology Colleges) Regulations 1987 (SI 1987 No. 138)
20. Education (Abolition of Corporal Punishment) (Independent Schools) Regulations 1987 (SI 1987 No. 1183)
21. Pupils' Registration (Amendment) Regulations 1987 (SI 1987 No. 1285)
22. Education (School Government) Regulations 1987 (SI 1987 No. 1359)
23. Education (School Teachers' Pay and Conditions) Order 1987 (SI 1987 No. 650)

## CIRCULARS AND ADMINISTRATIVE MEMORANDA

1. DES Circular 7/74 (14.6.74) *Work Experience*
2. DES Circular 11/78 (18.8.78) (amended by Circular 7/82) *Medical fitness of teachers and of entrants to training*
3. Circular 8/81 (7.12.81) *Education Act 1981*
4. DES Administrative Memorandum 3/82 (6.9.82) *Misconduct of Teachers*
5. DES Circular 1/83 (31.1.83) *Assessments and statements of special educational needs*
6. DES Circular letter (16.6.83) *Placement of Children with Statements at Independent Schools*
7. DES Circular 6/83 (2.11.83) *The approval of special schools*
8. DES Circular 5/85 (Addendum) *Education Support* (20.12.85) *Grants: Midday supervision in schools*
9. DES Circular 4/86 (17.7.86) *Protection of children: disclosure of criminal background of those with access to children*
10. DES Circular 8/86 (19.12.86) *Education (No. 2) Act 1986*
11. DES Circular 2/87 (17.3.87) *Education (Publication of Proposals to Change Status of a Controlled School) Regulations 1987*
12. DES Circular 3/87 (6.5.87) *Providing for quality: the pattern of organisation to age 19*
13. DES Circular No. 7/87 (7.8.87) *Education (No. 2) Act 1986: Further guidance*
14. DES Circular No. 11/87 (25.9.87) *Sex Education at School*

# Further Reading

*The Head's Legal Guide;* Croner Publications
*Reference Book for Employers;* Croner Publications
*Guide to Health and Safety;* Croner Publications
*Guide to Interviews;* Croner Publications
*The Education (No.2) Act 1986: Implications for School Management;* Chris Lowe; Secondary Heads Association (SHA)
*New School Government Regulations: Education Act 1986;* Chris Lowe; SHA
*Conditions of Employment: Implications for School Management;* John Sutton; SHA
*The Law of Education;* ed Peter Liell and John B Saunders; Butterworth
*Teachers and the Law;* G R Barrell and J A Partington; Methuen
*Data Protection Act 1984: Guideline No.1;* Data Protection Registrar
*The Effective School Governor;* Joan Sallis; Advisory Centre for Education (ACE)
*More Questions Governors Ask;* Joan Sallis; ACE
*The School in its Setting;* Joan Sallis; ACE
*School under threat;* Rick Rogers; ACE
*Education A-Z;* compiled by Elizabeth Wallis; ACE
*A Handbook for School Governors;* E C Wragg and J A Partington; Methuen
*School Governors;* Kenneth Brooksbank and Keith Anderson; Longman
*School Governors' Guide;* Barbara Bullivant; Home and School Council
*School Governors' Handbook and Training Guide;* Tyrell Burgess and Ann Sofer; Kogan Page
*Parental Influence at School;* (Green Paper Cmnd 9242 23.5.1984); HMSO
*A New Partnership for Schools (The Taylor Committee Report);* 1977; HMSO
*County and Voluntary Schools;* K Brooksbank et al; Councils and Education Press
*Towards Better Management of Secondary Education;* Audit Commission and the Industrial Society
*School Financial Management;* ed Peter Downes; Basil Blackwell
*Managing School Finance;* B A A Knight; Heineman Educational
*Curriculum 5-16;* (DES); HMSO
*Curriculum 11-16: Towards a Statement of Entitlement;* (DES); HMSO
*GCSE General Criteria;* DES 1985
*Education Observed No.5 "Good Behaviour and Discipline in Schools";* DES 1987
*Safety Policies in the Education Sector;* HMSO
*DES Safety series 1 to 6;* Architects and Building Group; DES
*Special Educational Needs:* Report of the Committee of Enquiry into the Education of Handicapped Children and Young People (The Warnock Report); HMSO

*Disclosure of Information to Trade Unions for Collective Bargaining Purposes;* Advisory
   Conciliation and Arbitration Service (ACAS)
*Public Entertainment Licensing and School Premises;* Home Office Statement; May 1984
*Liaison between the Police and Schools;* Association of Chief Police Officers and Society of
   Education Officers
*Working Together for a Better Future;* DES and Dept of Employment
*Education for All;* The Swann Report 1985; HMSO
*Better Schools;* (Cmnd 9469 March 1985); HMSO
*Aspects of Secondary Education in England;* A Survey by HM Inspectors of Schools; HMSO

## JOURNALS

School Governor; 73 All Saints Road Birmingham B14 7LN
Parents and Schools; Campaign for the Advancement of State Education (CASE)
Home and School; National Confederation of Parent-Teacher Associations

## VIDEO TAPES

On being a School Governor;
I'm Not Satisfied, Mr Barlow;
School Exclusions Explored;
Focus in Education Ltd
65 High Street
Hampton Hill
Middlesex TW12 1NH

# Useful
# Addresses

Advisory Conciliation and Arbitration Service
(ACAS)
11-12 St James's Square
London SW1Y 4LA
01-210 3600

Advisory Centre for Education
18 Victoria Park Square
London E2 9PB
01-980 4596

Assessment of Performance Unit (APU)
DES
Elizabeth House
York Road
London SE1 7PH
01-934 9323

Buddhist Society
58 Eccleston Square
London SW1V 1PH
01-834 5858

Campaign for the Advancement of State
Education (CASE)
The Grove
110 High Street
Sawston
Cambridgeshire CB2 4HJ
0223 833179

Careers Research Advisory Council
Bateman Street
Cambridge CB2 1LZ
0223 354551

Catholic Education Council
41 Cromwell Road
London SW7 2DJ
01-584 7491

Central Arbitration Committee
15-17 Ormond Yard
Duke of York Street
London SW1Y 6JT
01-214 3048

Central Bureau for Educational Visits and
Exchanges
Seymour Mews House
Seymour Mews
London W1H 9PE
01-486 5101

Chartered Institute of Public Finance and
Accountancy (CIPFA)
3 Robert Street
London WC2N 6BH
01-930 3456

Charity Commission (London)
14 Ryder Street
St James's Square
London SW1Y 6AH
01-214 6000

Children's Legal Centre
20 Compton Terrace
London N1 2UN
01-359 6251

Church of England Board of Education
Church House
Dean's Yard
London SW1P 3NZ
01-222 9011

Civic Trust Heritage Education Trust
17 Carlton House Terrace
London SW17 5AW
01-930 0914

Commission for Racial Equality
Elliot House
10-12 Allington Street
London SW1E 5EH
01-828 7022

Commission of the European Communities
200 rue de la Loi
1049 Bruxelles
Belgium

Council of Europe
Directorate of Education
CEDEX
67006 Strasbourg
France

Council for Education in World Citizenship
19-21 Tudor Street
London EC4Y 0DJ
01-353 3353

Council of Local Education Authorities
Eaton House
66a Eaton Square
Westminster
London SW1W 9BH
01-235 1200

Council for National Academic Awards
344-354 Gray's Inn Road
London WC1X 8BP
01-278 4411

Criminal Injuries Compensation Board
Wittington House
19-30 Alfred Place
Chenies Street
London WC1 7EJ
01-636 2812

Data Protection Registrar
Springfield House
Water Lane
Wilmslow
Cheshire SK9 5AX
0625 535777

Department of Education and Science
Elizabeth House
York Road
London SE1 7PH
01-934 9000

Department of Employment
Administrative Headquarters
Caxton House
Tothill Street
London SW1H 9NF
01-273 3000

Education Alliance
Congress House
Great Russell Street
London WC1B 3LS

Education National Industries Group
Maritime House
1 Linton Road
Barking
Essex IG11 8HF
01-594 5522

"Education Otherwise"
25 Common Lane
Hemmingford Abbots
Cambridgeshire TF18 9AN

Employment Appeal Tribunal
4 St James's Square
London SW1Y 4JU
01-210 3000

Equal Opportunities Commission
Overseas House
Quay Street
Manchester M3 3HN
061-833 9244

Focus in Education Ltd (Videos for
  Governors)
65 High Street
Hampton Hill
Middlesex TW12 1NH
01-783 0333

Governing Bodies' Association (also
  Governing Bodies' of Girls Schools
  Association)
The Flat
The Lambdens
Beenham
Berkshire RG7 5JY

HM Inspector of Taxes
Inland Revenue Claims Branch
Charity Division
St John's House
Merton Road
Bootle
Merseyside L69 9BB
051-922 6363

Health Education Council
78 New Oxford Street
London WC1A 1AH
01-631 0930

Health and Safety Commission
Regina House
259-269 Old Marylebone Road
London NW1 5RR
01-723 1262

Health and Safety Executive
St Hugh's House
Stanley Precinct
Bootle
Merseyside L20 3QY
051-951 4000

Her Majesty's Stationery Office (HMSO)
49 High Holborn
London WC1V 6HB
01-211 5656

HMSO (Birmingham)
258 Broad Street
Birmingham B1 2HE
021-643 3757

HMSO (Bristol)
33 Wine Street
Bristol BS1 2BQ
0272 24306

Hindu Centre
39 Grafton Terrace
London NW5
01-485 8200

Independent Schools Information Service
   (ISIS)
56 Buckingham Gate
London SW1E 6AG
01-630 8793

Insurance Brokers' Registration Council
15 St Helens Place
London EC3A 6DS
01-588 4387

Islamic Cultural Centre and London Central
   Mosque
146 Park Road
London NW8
01-724 3363

Industrial Society
3 Carlton House Terrace
London SW1 5DG
01-839 4300

Jewish Education Bureau
8 Westcombe Avenue
Leeds LS8 2BS
0532 663613

Justices' Clerks' Society
Magistrates' Court
PO Box 107
Nelson Street
Bristol BS99 7BJ
0272 297841

Law Society
The Law Society's Hall
113 Chancery Lane
London WC2A 1PL
01-242 1222

London Diocesan Board for Schools
30 Causton Street
London SW1P 4AU
01-821 9311

Manpower Services Commission
Selkirk House
166 High Holborn
London WC1V 6PF
01-836 1213

National Association of Governors and
   Managers (NAGM)
81 Rustlings Road
Sheffield S11 7AB
0742 662467

NAGM Educational Research Trust
10 Brookfield Park
London NW5 1ER
01-485 4258

National Advisory Unit for Community
   Transport
Keymer Street
Beswick
Manchester M11 3FY
061-273 6038

National Council for Special Education
1 Wood Street
Stratford upon Avon CV37 6JE
0789 205332

National Education Association
18 Bisham Gardens
London N6
01-340 2359

National Foundation for Educational
  Research in England and Wales
The Mere
Upton Park
Slough
Buckinghamshire SL1 2DQ
0753 74123

National Confederation of Parent-Teacher
  Associations
43 Stonebridge Road
Northfleet
Gravesend
Kent DA11 9DS
0474 60618

Parent Teacher Association of Wales
Publicity Officer
Tolgoed Pen y Lon
Mynydd Isa
Mold
Clwyd CH7 6YG
0352 4652

Royal Society for the Prevention of Accidents
Cannon House
Priory Queensway
Birmingham B4 6BS
021-233 2461

School Journey Association of London
48 Cavendish Road
London SW12 0DH
01-673 4849

Schools Computer Development Centre
Birchover Road
Bilborough
Nottingham

School Curriculum Development Committee
Newcombe House
45 Notting Hill Gate
London W11 3JB
01-229 1234

Secondary Examinations Council
Newcombe House
45 Notting Hill Gate
London W11 3JB
01-229 1234

Secondary Heads Association
Chancery House
107 St Paul's Road
London NW1 2NB
01-359 9286

Sikh Cultural Society of Great Britain
88 Mollison Way
Edgware
London HA8 5QW
01-952 1215

Standing Conference on Drug Abuse
1-4 Hatton Place
Hatton Garden
London EC1N 8ND
01-430 2341

Trades Union Congress
23-28 Great Russell Street
London WC1B 3LS
01-636 4030

# Index